You Are Not Alone

True Stories of Sexual Assault, Abuse, & Harassment from Around the World

By Jyssica Schwartz

Copyright © 2018 by Jyssica Schwartz.

All rights reserved. No part of this publication may be reproduced, distributed, or transmitted in any form or by any means, including photocopying, recording, or other electronic or mechanical methods, without the prior written permission of the publisher, except in the case of brief quotations embodied in critical reviews and certain other noncommercial uses permitted by copyright law. For permission requests, write to the author at the address below.

jyssica.schwartz@gmail.com

Disclaimer: All stories in this book are printed and published with permission from the individual writers. In many cases, both the writer's names and the names of the perpetrators have been changed to protect victims from retaliation or recognition. All stories have been freely donated to be included in this anthology.

10% of proceeds from all sales of this book is going to the **RAINN** organization.

Edited by Amy Blocher & William Blocher
Interior Formatting & Design by Angela Buer
Cover Design by Christos Angelidakis

Dedication

This project is a collection of freely-contributed stories in their own words from women and men around the world of their experiences with sexual assault, abuse, and harassment. Some are short, a few long, a couple are poems, and all are real.

The purpose of this book is to continue to allow people to speak their truth, to stand up, and speak out.

It's about keeping the conversation going and not allowing the #metoo movement to fade into the background, the world content to continue to let abusers and harassers off the hook.

It is about refusing to be a part of victim-blaming, slut-shaming, and staying quiet to "keep the peace." The victims of sexual assault, abuse, and harassment hold on to their shame and discomfort, feeling as though it is their fault, and it is time to stop allowing victims to shoulder the responsibility for their abuse.

This book is for everyone who has kept their secrets for too long.

Thank you for having the strength to reveal these atrocities and bring them to light, to finally know it is not your fault, and to know you are not alone.

You are not alone.

Table of Contents

Introduction	1
Jyssica, 31, New York, USA - My Story	5
Lisa, 58, Missouri, USA	8
Karen, 55, Pennsylvania, USA	10
Lisa C., 53, New Jersey, USA	14
Leticia, 20, Spain	15
Megan, 20, Oregon, USA	19
Michelle, 30, California, USA	20
Ryan, 35, Massachusetts, USA	27
Amanda, 32, Toronto, Canada	29
Angela, 45, California, USA	30
Theresa, 21, North Carolina, USA	34
Mae, 30, Florida, USA	35
Julia Freifeld - #MeToo Original Song	42
B, 30, Arizona, USA	44
Josh, 43, California, USA	46
Mandy, 32, Florida, USA	53
Rachael C., 39, Gold Coast, Australia	55
Anonymous Twitter Story	62
Helena, 68, Portugal	63
Samantha, 20, Minnesota, USA	67
Ann, 70, Missouri, USA	69
J.M., 48, New York, USA	70
Mark, 62, New York, USA	76
Alexis, 18, Pennsylvania, USA	78
Marita M., 56, Victoria, Australia	81
Leta. 34, California, USA	89
Anonymous, 14, Minnesota, USA	91
Melissa D., 65, New York, USA	92
Sharine, 54, California, USA	96

Michelle, Age 36, Texas, USA	103
Michael L., 72 years old, Kansas, USA	105
Renee, 48, Arizona, USA	110
Apolonia, 31, Florida, USA	112
Carolyn M., Toronto, Canada	116
Monet, 35, New York, USA	118
Carol R. T., 70, Kentucky, USA	122
Kee, 19, California, USA	123
Crystal, 43, Ohio, USA	129
Bob, 62, New York, USA	131
Linda, 58, Oklahoma, USA	136
Madeleine Black, 52, Glasgow, Scotland	137
Kim, 55, Indiana, USA	141
Charity, 27, Arizona, USA	142
Julie, 17, California, USA	147
Tamara, 40, California, USA	149
Ella, 19, Aarhus, Denmark	151
Khalid, 30, United Arab Emirates	153
Lisa, 44, New Jersey, USA	156
Ava, 32, California, USA	158
Jenn, 21, Maryland, USA	161
Mel, 15, Ohio, USA	163
Luna, 16, Netherlands	166
Emily, 20, Vermont, USA	167
Matthew L., 33, Texas, USA	168
Misty Griffin, 35, California, USA	171
Conclusion	174
Statistics	175
Resources	177
Bios	179
Historical Feminist Figures - List	181

Introduction

Tarana Burke is an activist and a sexual violence survivor. In 2007, after years of listening to and helping young women who were victims of sexual assault and abuse, Burke created Just Be, Inc., a nonprofit organization to help these victims. Burke became an advocate for victims and named her movement "Me Too." She has become a vocal and inspiring head of this movement, which originally focused on bringing victims of color to a place where their voices were heard and has now expanded to include all victims.

Ten years later, on October 15, 2017, actress Alyssa Milano simply wanted to give a voice to sexual abuse victims when she tweeted out a photo which said "Me too. Suggested by a friend: 'If all the women who have been sexually harassed or assaulted wrote 'me too' as a status, we might give people a sense of the magnitude of the problem.'"

The magnitude of the response across all social media platforms was incredible and immediate. On Facebook alone, the message was shared more than 12 million times in the first 24 hours and spurred millions of responses on Twitter, Facebook, Instagram and more over the next months.

When being interviewed by Robin Roberts on "Good Morning America," Milano said, "What the 'Me Too' campaign really does, and what Tarana Burke has really enabled us to do, is put the focus back on the victims."

As the #metoo movement grew, more people around the world found the courage to share their stories - many of them for the very first time.

Burke wants to focus on the systems in place which have previously allowed sexual violence to continue to flourish and to be kept hidden for so long.

"We often don't think about what happens after there's this groundswell of support," she said. "Everyone feels good about it in the moment, but then you have to sit with that disclosure after the fact. We're hoping to help people create a way to process after the hashtag."

Major news stations stayed on the #metoo movement and the news became filled with many more famous men being outed as abusers and harassers. The Harvey Weinstein scandal broke, the backlash to which forced Weinstein out of his own company. The Kevin Spacey scandal came to light, and the response was immediate: He was kicked off of his Netflix show "House of Cards," where he was the main character. The show is continuing to film its sixth season with an amazing Robin Wright taking the lead - long deserved.

Women who had hidden their abuse for most of their lives came forward to speak out and break their silence, earning the title "The Silence Breakers."

In a crescendo of the movement, The Silence Breakers were named the TIME Person of the Year for 2017, continuing to put this movement and its stories in the spotlight, highlighting their bravery and showing there is still much work to be done.

Unfortunately, Donald Trump was right behind The Silence Breakers in the running for being named TIME Person of the Year, proving yet again there is so much more which needs to happen to break our society out of the habit of quieting victims and allowing abuse of power and authority as an excuse. This is not to say Trump was second-most popular; TIME picks the person of the year based on impact made. This is how people such as Hitler, Stalin, Putin, and Ayatollah Khomeini have been named Person of the year previously.

When asked why some victims waited so long to come forward, there have been many reasons given. But it truly comes down to the fear of being blamed and shamed.

When a woman is raped, the questions begin. "What were you wearing?" "Were you drinking?" "Where were you?" "Did you flirt with him?"

As if wearing a low-cut shirt is simply an invitation to have your rights as a human being and your autonomy violated.

As if drinking a beer is an advertisement that you want forced sex.
As if walking home from a bar is an invitation to be followed, harassed, or attacked.

It is time this ended.

Feminists do not hate men. They don't even want to take anything from them. They simply want the same equality, rights, and benefits afforded to them as the men in the world.

And if this somehow threatens you? Then that is your fault, not ours.

While accepting the Cecil B. DeMille award at the 2018 Golden Globes, Oprah Winfrey used her moment in the spotlight to bring the #Metoo movement and the #TimesUp initiative to the forefront of the night, saying, "What I know for sure is that speaking your truth is the most powerful tool we all have, and I am especially proud and inspired by all the women who have felt strong enough and empowered enough to speak up and share their personal stories. ... Each of us is empowered and celebrated because of the stories that we tell."

Time's Up is a unified call for change from women in the entertainment industry. Time's Up manages a legal defense fund aimed at helping underprivileged women fight against sexual harassment, assault, and retaliation. Powered by women and completely volunteer-led, Time's Up addresses the systematic inequality and injustice in the workplace which has kept underrepresented groups from reaching their full potential, and advocates for a significant increase of women in leadership positions across all industries. Many famous actors and actresses have donated and become involved. As of Monday, January 8, 2018, the legal defense fund had raised more than $16 million in 18 days.

As the #metoo movement continues to swell and move across the world, as more women and men around the world break their silence, stand up, and speak out, we are continuing to say that we will no longer stand for hiding our pain and keeping quiet about our experiences.

My name is Jyssica Schwartz. I have been assaulted, harassed, followed, and commented on. I am done wondering if it was something I did or something I said to provoke these incidents. I am finished tucking them away and thinking "that is just how the world is."

I am done sitting on the sidelines, and seeing and hoping other people would make the changes for the rest of us.

This book has been an extreme labor of love. I have gotten the absolute pleasure of meeting and speaking to survivors who have created lives worth living, who have gone on healing paths, spoken their truth, and keep living outside of the shadows.

This book has 56 stories from women and men who were willing to come forward and donate their experiences in order to break their silence and to help others. The stories came from contributors as young as 14 years old to as old as 72. There are stories from Spain, Russia, Portugal, Denmark, United Arab Emirates, Australia, Netherlands, Canada, and all over the United States.

They are stories of survival. They are stories of the depths to which some people go, uncaring of how they affect others or whom they hurt. They are stories of predators and victims.

These are victims who are no longer willing to bear their experiences in silence.

The brave women and men who make up this book are amazing. From the bottom of my soul, thank you for participating in this project. Thank you, readers, for seeing these people as more than victims, but as who they really are: Survivors. Advocates. Mothers. Daughters. Sons. Friends.

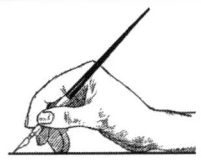

Jyssica, 31, New York, USA - My Story

Once it started, my social media feeds were full of #metoo posts from women around the world.

As I watched the flood of posts, scrolling past another and another, then more and more, my heart broke a little more each time. Every woman I know on Facebook, strangers on Twitter, celebrities stepping forward for the first time, I felt the heat start to rise in my chest.

While #metoo was provoking conversation and forcing men and perpetrators to see the actual human beings in their lives who have been personally affected by sexual harassment, it should not have been even remotely a surprise.

Be sad, make promises, be horrified, but don't lie to us and say you're surprised.

America is a nation which blames the victim of sexual assault more often than not. 99 percent of sexual violence perpetrators walk free. School dress codes say girls have to cover their shoulders so the BOYS can learn; this is a world in which some countries just don't permit girls to go to school during their period week. Or not at all.

In a world where my uterus is federally regulated, where it's harder to get an abortion than a gun, you are not allowed to be surprised that every woman you know has been harassed or assaulted, and most of them so many times they simply shrug it off.

We stop telling people.

Girls are taught to carry pepper spray, wear different and more modest clothes, never put down your drink, don't go out alone at night, carry your keys so they stick out from between each finger, just in case.

Women are scared to walk alone in parking garages or late at night in their own neighborhood. We base decisions about how late to stay out, the outfit we wear, and where we park our car all on the possibility of harassment or assault.

Me too. Of course, me too.

Me too because I had a "friend" follow me back to my apartment after a party in college and try to force himself on me. He said I had flirted with him and clearly wanted him or else I "wouldn't have worn that." Because this happened more than once.

Me too because I have been groped on NYC trains, at parties, and in lines.

Me too because I can't walk down the street after dark without feeling extremely vulnerable and nervous. Without walking faster and holding my purse a little tighter and hunching my shoulders or sticking out my belly - to look less appealing and to try to be invisible.

Me too because men feel like it's okay to tell me to "smile" or comment loudly on my weight or my breasts or my clothes as I walk in their general vicinity.

Me too because I grew up knowing I have to fear rape and assault from men who are bigger than me, and have to make daily decisions based on the fact that simply because I am a woman, I am far more likely to be physically and sexually assaulted.

I am happy the #metoo movement is opening men's eyes to the true epidemic of harassment, rape and assault, and how it makes women feel.

But the fact is that we needed to have a movement so that half the population would even be aware that women are their own individual humans and should not be left in daily indoctrinated fear.

When will our society move from "here is how you can protect yourself from assault, ladies" to "men, do not assault. This is your responsibility and you will be held accountable for your actions"?

At what point will we stop blaming the victims and start realizing no matter what someone is wearing, drinking, or where they happen to be at any particular moment, "no" means NO, STOP THAT? That women are humans who deserve personal space, autonomy, and not to be violated, assaulted, abused, or harassed simply for existing. When will men begin to realize we are people, too?

And it infuriates me when people say they understand "because I have a daughter/sister/mother, etc." Why can't people be a decent human being without needing to have a family member remind you to do so?

So, yes, #MeToo.

Adam Jones - Political scientist and active feminist at the University of British Columbia Okanagan. He wrote "Gender Inclusive: Essays on Violence, Men, and Feminist International Relations," 2009, Routledge. His "Gendercide Watch" website is dedicated to documenting gender-selective mass killing.

Lisa, 58, Missouri, USA

One Experience of Sexual Assault - My First Foray into Therapy

1980's. I was dealing with quite a lot: My career path was unsure despite years of study, my love life was in tatters, I was feeling unappreciated in a work situation, and the aftermath of coming out to my parents was pretty horrendous. I was a bit depressed.

The college had free counseling. I signed up.

My first experience with counseling was with S, a tall, thin, geeky guy. During our first session, he asked a lot of questions and listened intently. I decided he was okay and agreed to return the next week. In the second session, he asked more questions, but they were all about my sexuality and sexual experiences. He kept pushing for details and I kept telling him that I would not discuss these things.

Then he said, "Your problem is that you're not a real woman. You're a scared little virgin. So you think that you don't want men. You don't have to be scared. It won't hurt. I can fix this for you." While rubbing my shoulders.

I was completely speechless for a moment, but recovered. I stood up to face him and to make him stop touching me. I replied that I had never felt any physical attraction to any male. Ever. I reminded him that he could be thrown out of the program for physical contact. I asked if I should go to the director and quit the program.

He laughed. He said he would tell everyone I was a lying stupid dyke who was mentally unstable. He said I only had to try it one time. He was the cure. He grabbed me, pushed me against the wall, pulled on my shirt (which lost some buttons), and started kissing me.

Now, at this time I was working in a karate school and I was in great shape. I punched as hard as I could into his solar plexus, bloodied his nose, then left him on all fours on the floor. Then I went to the director of the program and told her exactly why I hit him.

The director called a day later and told me that she had spoken to S. He would only work with male clients for the rest of the semester. She wanted me to come in and meet M - a female counselor. M was really good, actually. And she would walk me to the door, so when we saw S in the hall and he snarled insults and threats, we always responded with "Shut up, S." The director heard some of these and joined us, "Yeah, shut up, S."

M and I were a bit irritated, though, that the only disciplinary action S received was to be denied female clients for a few months. We agreed the slimeball would probably, someday, get female clients to do his bidding. But hey, that just happens, right?

Maybe my orientation helped me deal with my few experiences of sexual assault. I never experienced any "maybe I led him on" guilt. I most certainly never led any guy on! And each time I went from "what?" to "KILL!!!!!" so fast that the only emotion associated with these instances is fury. I suppose I'm lucky.

What would I do differently now? Turn on my phone to record the conversation? Call the police? It would have been difficult to prove that he assaulted me without a recording. But I would definitely be more assertive with the director.

#

Alice Stone Blackwell – Known for her lifelong fight for women's rights, Blackwell became a prominent reformer with Susan B. Anthony and Elizabeth Cady Stanton. She was the daughter of two suffrage leaders who helped establish the American Woman Suffrage Association. "The Woman's Journal," a paper started by her parents, fell to her responsibility and sole editorial discretion. In 1890, she helped to combine the two competing women's suffrage organizations into one called the National American Woman Suffrage Association (NAWSA), serving as both secretary and national auditor from 1890-1910.

Karen, 55, Pennsylvania, USA

My name is Karen. My father began molesting me when I was just 4 years old.

My father is a pedophile and my mother is a narcissistic, emotionally unavailable alcoholic. She stopped drinking when I was 17, but never stopped medicating herself. I basically raised myself.

I also believe my mother knew about the abuse and never did anything because of her own pride or embarrassment. I told her what happened when I was in my 20s, and her response was to tell me not to tell my uncles. She never asked how I was or spoke about it again. She did, however, tell my stepsister without my consent.

I was born in Buffalo, NY, to an unmarried woman and a man I know very little about. My parents married a month after I was born, but my mother and I lived with her parents and two of her brothers until I was 4 years old. I was a happy, healthy, and loved little girl. My grandfather and my uncles spoiled me rotten. I would learn much later in life that my mother's other brother and his wife had wanted to adopt me, but my mother wouldn't allow it.

When I was 4, we moved to Delaware County, Pennsylvania, first living with my father's parents and then in a house of our own. That's when it began. I went from a fully-loved and adored little girl to a thing. I don't remember the trauma of being torn away from the people who loved me and shoved into hell, but I do remember being frightened most of the time.

It doesn't really matter what he did, what matters is that he violated my little-girl trust and stole my innocence. My parents divorced when I was 6, but I was still required to visit him until I was 11 or 12. I hated those visits. The molestation didn't stop until I said no.

My father was in a motorcycle gang and was house-sitting for his sister and he brought me along. While sitting in a room full of people, he caught my eye, pointed at his crotch, and raised his eyebrows. I knew exactly what he meant. I shook my head and ran out of the room.

I never saw him again. He knew that I knew and understood.

I remember very little from those years except that I had stomach problems. I always felt sick. My mother would take me to the doctor and he would tell me to take antacids. I lived on them. Now I know why, and hope adults have learned to recognize the health signs of prolonged abuse.

As a teenager, I became promiscuous, looking for love the only way I knew. I spent most of my teenage years drinking and trying drugs. Someone must have been watching over me, because I should be dead.

As a young adult, I was self-medicating and an emotional mess. At some point, I realized that what had happened to me was wrong and shameful. As I've heard so many women say, it was my story. It was a story with no emotions, almost like a play of my life which I watched over and over.

I got married when I was 26 and had two children by the time I was 30. I realized that if I wanted to be a good mother, I had to finally deal with my issues.

My first attempt at getting help was an ACOA class, since my mother was an alcoholic, and I thought most of my problems came from that. It was a start, and led to 20 years of therapy with two wonderful women who made me see I needed to accept, care for, and love that little girl who no one had ever loved or taken care of: me.

I have always suffered from depression, sometimes deep, deep depression, but I've survived. And I like to think I'm thriving. When I was 25, I had no idea what made me sad, because I had no idea how to identify how I felt or how to get to the root of my sadness. I had the typical response to abuse in that I suppressed both good and bad feelings, and had no idea how to identify them.

I remember having a paper with faces for each expression and trying to figure out which one fit my moods.

The depression still simmers today, but I know how to deal with it now. I bring it out and play with it. I was never a good candidate for antidepressants, though I did try them for six months during a very bad time and they did help.

My husband is the best thing that ever happened to me. He has been kind and patient for almost 30 years now. It took a long time for me to trust him with my feelings, but he's always been there for me.

I am who I am because of where I've been. I am extremely empathetic, I "feel" everyone's energy all the time. It's exhausting. I'm hypervigilant from always being aware and afraid of what was happening in my own house when I was a child. I have PTSD and I hate being touched without warning.

I've learned to use all of these things to my advantage or to work around them. Empathy is a gift. I know when you're hurting and I'll call you on it. I know when someone needs a hug and when someone needs to be left alone. I've turned hypervigilance into "stop and smell the roses" – I never miss a beautiful gift from Nature. I've learned to hug those I love and to set physical and emotional boundaries with those I don't. I am not afraid to tell someone not to touch me. "Not a hugger" is a very useful phrase when someone attempts to touch you without your permission! I've had three coworkers touch me inappropriately, all men, and all put in their places immediately. It's my body and I choose who gets to touch it!!

All of the people who wonder why it took so long for anyone, any victim, to speak up should know these things:
1.	Being a victim of sexual abuse makes the victim feel ashamed until she, or he, can understand it was not her/his fault. Some victims never get to that point.
2.	Many victims are threatened with harm or even death if they tell.
3.	There are still many idiots who blame the victim, making it scary to come forward.
4.	Victims are often not believed in the first place, which makes it

harder for them to speak out.
5. Many victims have a deep fear of being ignored, deserted, embarrassed, and losing social status, friends, family, and more.
6. Victims often feel dirty and not worthy of love.

My father probably suffered some sort of abuse himself. I don't think pedophiles are born; I believe they're made. He is still alive and will probably never be held accountable for what he did, and I truly regret that. I never realized or thought about it until writing this, but it seems clear to me now that the only reason my father exercised his visitation rights was to molest me. That realization is especially painful.

What I don't regret is that I have stopped the cycle. My children are happy, healthy, good people who love me as I love them. I'm very proud of them and hope they're proud of me.

They say the first few years of a child's life are critical to their emotional development. I believe that with all my heart. My grandfather loved me unconditionally, which gave me some sort of soul and saved me. Then later, my husband gave me the love and support of a good man, and a friend to help me to live a good, mostly happy life.

One last thing for those of you who think you don't know someone who's been abused, think again. They're often right next door and hiding in plain sight.

If you see something, SAY SOMETHING!
#MeToo

Alison Bechdel —An American cartoonist best known for her comic strip "Dykes to Watch Out For." In 2006, she wrote her graphic memoir "Fun Home" and it was adapted as a musical, winning the Tony Award for Best Musical in 2015. Core messages in her work include gender non-conformity and her sexuality as a lesbian. "The secret subversive goal of my work is to show that women, not just lesbians, are regular human beings."

Lisa C., 53, New Jersey, USA

Telling the Story She Won't

She was smart. She was beautiful. She was sexy. She never tried hard at being any of those things. They came naturally. It was 1963 and she was one of those working women. Her boss required her to wear a skirt or a dress to work. Pants were not an option.

As she rode the subway into Manhattan from Brooklyn to her job while wearing her skirt, a man seated on the subway car reached under her skirt and grabbed her vagina. Shocked and scared, she went to work, cried, and discussed the situation with her husband. Soon after, she quit her job. She may have quit sooner or later, anyway, since she was pregnant, but that is not the point.

That woman was my mother. I believe her.

Alyssa Milano — Milano was one of the accounts to first tweet a message encouraging survivors of sexual harassment and assault to post #metoo as a status. She engaged her followers and was inspired by the overwhelming response to bring awareness to the commonality of sex crimes among women in the wake of H. Weinstein's expulsion from the Academy of Motion Picture Arts and Sciences for alleged sex crimes against women in the industry (2017). She helped to create a platform where women have an opportunity to tell their stories. She and Tarana Burke are continuing to promote change.

Leticia, 20, Spain

The Bartenders

It all started in July 2017. I like to go out with friends and have a few drinks, especially at this one rooftop bar next to the beach. All of the bartenders were good-looking, but I especially liked one of them. I started to get drinks at his bar and made some remarks about his looks, and I flirted with him. And he had his fun with me, too. He always took a shot with me and said it was on the house.

It started to be "normal" to go to his bar. Sometimes it was his friend who served me, and he always hit on me and my friends, too. They were both your typical bartenders who liked to flirt with girls, but that is all it was - just a little bartender-flirting for tips and to make us laugh.

At the end of August, a friend from another country came to visit me for a week. We went out on a Saturday, as usual to that one rooftop bar with the cute bartenders. I didn't drink a lot that night. Just one beer and one gin & tonic. But I was so drunk I can't remember some things from that night.

The next day, I just thought that I probably hadn't eaten enough or something like that. But looking back to it, I think someone put something in my drink, because it was just impossible for me to have been so drunk.

On my friend's last night visiting, we went out again, to the same rooftop bar. It was a Wednesday and there weren't a lot of people there, not like on a Friday or Saturday. We had a couple drinks, but nothing much. The two bartenders who had flirted with me since July were "focused" on us. They wanted us to take drinks with them and stay at their bar. That's what we did, we liked the admiration. They told us to come to one of their houses after their shift and have a "Café noir."

My friend absolutely wanted to go, but I didn't, because I felt like it wasn't a good idea. When their shifts ended, my friend insisted on going to their house. She told me, "Come on! They're hot! And they live near your house and we'll just stay for 10 minutes!"

I gave up on saying no.

So, she went in the car of the one I had been admiring since July (whom I will call "Gold") and I went in the other bartender's car. We didn't talk a lot, and we smoked a cigarette (something I rarely do).

When we were at his house, my friend and my crush started to make out. I was feeling bad and I didn't want to do anything with them, so I just sat on the couch and waited until we could go home. My friend and Gold were starting to undress. Then, let's call the other one "Rubin," asked me if I wanted to do the same. I told him no. He accepted that answer. My friend and Gold went to the bedroom.

Rubin went to the kitchen and I followed him because I wanted to drink some water. He took something out of a cupboard, a little plastic bag with white powder. I asked him what it was, he told me, "Cocaine, do you want some?" I told him no, I never take drugs. He was making himself a line of cocaine and I was drinking my water and I started to walk out of the kitchen.

Suddenly he grabbed my hand and said: "Take some!" I repeated myself and said I didn't want to. He started to pull me over to him and said with an angry voice, "Take some, little bitch!"

I felt anxious. I wanted to walk away, but he grabbed my head harshly and slammed it on the kitchen counter and said "Sniff! Sniff! Take it!"

I couldn't move anymore because he hurt me. I tried to defend myself, but I couldn't, so I sniffed. I felt as it went up my head and it tickled me in all my body. He let go of me and I jumped away, "Are you insane? I told you I didn't want to!" He didn't say anything anymore, just took his line and went back to the couch.

I went to the door of the bedroom where my friend was with Gold and knocked on the door and yelled, "Let's go home! Immediately!" She said that she's coming.

I suddenly felt like I didn't have control over my body and sat down on the couch in front of Rubin. The door of the bedroom opened and Gold came out of the room, naked, with a boner and he said, "Your friend is boring, she fell asleep!" The other one saw him and jumped over and grabbed my arms, so I couldn't move. Gold started to undress me, I couldn't move, I couldn't do anything to defend myself. Rubin grabbed my arms and feet so that I couldn't move at all.

This part is a little blurry, and I don't know if it's because I was kind of knocked out or just because I want to forget it.

I suddenly realized I was naked, and I couldn't move at all. Rubin came up to my mouth and put his dick in my mouth, so deep I felt like I was going to vomit. Gold was starting to penetrate me. Then Rubin kissed me with violence and he grabbed my face, opened my mouth and spat into my mouth three times.

I just wanted to cry.

I don't know how, but they moved me, and they started to both penetrate me, one in the front and the other in the back. I have never felt a pain like that in my life. I wanted to defend myself, but it was like my body wasn't mine. I shouted, so they made me silent by putting a penis violently in my mouth. They grabbed me everywhere and did with me what they wanted. My body was numb.

After some time, my friend came out of the room in just underwear and a t-shirt. Gold let go of me, because he probably didn't want her to see what they were doing to me. She said she heard me screaming. That was the moment when I could escape their violent hands. I stood up and started to call all possible male friends. No one answered the phone because it was 5 a.m.

Finally, after calling six other friends, one answered the phone. I told him to come pick us up and sent him the location. The boys calmed down because I told them someone was coming to get us, and if they touched us again, I would call the police. I had already dialled the number. We started to dress ourselves and went out of the apartment.

My friend was outside, and I was right behind her, but Rubin grabbed me and pulled me inside again and closed the door. He was still naked. Gold pulled me down and they both started to force their penises into my mouth. I didn't know what to do, so I just tried to bite them.

I don't know how much time went by, but my friend who came to pick us up was ringing at the door and yelled that he's going to break the door if they don't let go of me. I don't know how or when, but they finally let me out of the apartment. They closed the door. My friend carried me on his arm and brought me to the car where my other friend was already sitting. He brought us home safe.

Just recently, I talked to my friend who was with me, she hadn't realized what happened when she was in the room and the two guys were raping me because she had passed out. I never told her the whole story.

This is the first time that I'm telling this whole story. My parents didn't know anything, and neither do the police. No one knew anything. I felt ashamed of myself; I blamed myself for being too dumb and going home with them. I gave myself the fault for it, because I was too naïve. I never found the courage to tell this story.

And I still think that it's my own fault; I was the dumb one, and I should have known better. It's been some months now, but I'm still recovering. I don't have any sexual contact with men; every time someone grabs me I'm afraid. I'm afraid in the dark, and I see Gold and Rubin everywhere I go. I have a scar on my neck, from when Rubin grabbed me and forced my head down to take the cocaine. I'm thinking of moving to another place where I don't know anyone and where there's no risk of seeing them again. I have told all my friends to NEVER go home with guys, you never know who they are.

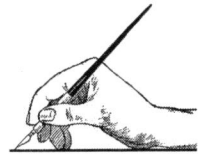

Megan, 20, Oregon, USA

When I was 16 years old, I was sexually assaulted.

I was with a few friends and we decided it would be fun to drink. I'll call the friends Sarah, Kyle, and Brett. This was my first time drinking.

After a couple hours, I was quite drunk and tired, and I decided to lay down. Kyle and Sarah were off doing their own thing, but Brett decided to lay down next to me. Then Brett started putting his hand in my pants. And then he put my hand in his. You can assume what happened from there.

I tried to say no and push him away from me, but I didn't have the strength.

At the time, I was too scared to try to take him to court. It took me almost a year to tell my own mother what happened. I was embarrassed. When I told my mom, I had to do it over text when I wasn't with her, so that I didn't have to say it out loud or see her reaction in the moment.

She immediately said she wanted me to change schools. She didn't know what else to do.

For me, healing has involved talking about it. The thing is, in order to talk, I had to find people I could trust, which was hard. I wanted to keep it private, but I also didn't want to bottle it up. It mainly took time and acceptance.

Sometimes, even now, when I get intimate with a guy, I have flashbacks, or even if I don't think about it, my body will remember certain feelings. What's important for me is telling him ahead of time that things are a little different for me. After four years, it's something I've been able to move on from a little. But it will always be a major part of my past.

It still affects me today. But I've gotten stronger and I know I'm not alone.

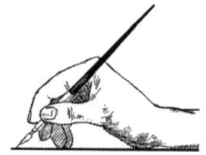

Michelle, 30, California, USA

He charmed me with his gifts and seemingly kind gestures. I saw it as thoughtful and kind, but Grandma warned me about that type. Perhaps he had a soft spot in his heart after all? I accepted him for who he was. His whole being. I gave grace to his journey and saw him as successful in many areas of his life.

But at some point, it didn't work for me. I had to walk away. It had become toxic. The apologies were just words. They had lost their meaning. The reality set in.

How did I let it get this far?

He was the kind of man everyone wanted to know.

He had bright blue-green eyes that sparkled when he smiled. He was Scandinavian (tall, strong, and handsome), and had this strong presence about him; everyone wanted to be around him. He had a way of finding out the little things about people and flattering them with his charm and a blink of his soft masculine eyelashes. He was, in many people's eyes, the "cool guy." Everyone wanted to know him or work him with him. He was, and is, a promoter for the reggae scene. A lot of the work he does is booking shows at venues around the states and a few internationally, and often tours with bands.

Making people feel good gave me a sense of belonging. I wanted everyday to just put a smile on someone's face. I became a licensed massage therapist. Maybe it got to me after decades of my dad dropping me off at school with a soft smile and nod saying, "Do something good for someone today, just because it feels good." Everyday was a day to become richer in love with life and everyone's story.

We had known each other for a few years: friends first, then lovers. It was near the end of the relationship when he started to reveal more of himself.

Specifically, there were times when he'd drink so much he'd black out. In the midst of having fun sometimes, he'd start to become angry, maybe not directly at me. He had revealed more from his past, prior to our relationship; he'd tell me his stories of running from cops, ex-girlfriends with restraining orders against him, carrying guns, stealing money, and as he liked to say, "riding on other people's coattails."

So, the "cool guy" was only one of his many sides.

He was always afraid of being "found out" as a liar by people. Many of his relationships, both personal and business, were imbalanced. Often people who owed him money or favors were too afraid to hold him accountable because of to his manipulative behavior and temper. Things I definitely didn't agree with.

Everyone has experiences and sometimes we carry them by tucking them away. Often we can stick to what we know as a means of survival, but it's not quite living. Our life and love can torment us if we carry our wounds and that can hurt other people. "Hurt people, hurt people." There could be any kind of trauma from childhood to adulthood which any one of us carries. I believe if somehow we could allow ourselves to process these things and go through the emotions running within us, the trauma can be released and our lives renewed. That can be a breakthrough! Life is a journey after all! But I could see the kind of trauma this guy was dealing with was far beyond what I could understand, and this one particular night became the end of us.

He booked a show one rainy night with an artist who he had toured with, and they were coming to play near our town. He was also the DJ that night and brought his own equipment to the venue. Once the show was over, I drove the truck around the back of the venue to load up everything. I couldn't find him anywhere. I called, no answer. He called back minutes later.

He accused me first thing, saying I ran away and tried to ditch him. I just listened to him yelling at me; there was no use in trying to defend myself in his drunken state. I finally got word that he rode the bus back with "the boys," somehow blaming me for his decision (what is called gaslighting). He was "telling me" I was never there and tried to escape from him. I thought he was delusional.

He tried to tell me how I was acting and who I was, when I'm thinking to myself, "You have got to be crazy." Someone is "telling me" something I did which never happened. I was there for him, but he believed his own story. I didn't understand why he had such a hard time looking at his own decisions. He yelled at me with every female-demeaning cuss word you could imagine. This lasted half an hour before the physical part ensued.

He tried grabbing the wheel of the truck while I was driving and pulling it back and forth from the passenger side. It got too much for me after he demanded to drive. I moved over to the passenger seat and he hopped in and sped off.

I remember so vividly my choice of not engaging with his manipulation. I tried to hold as firm as I could in my ability to be rational and logical in times of raging high emotions. But he got so angry that I remember his face turning bright red and his eyes popping out of his skull like he was going to kill me. I was so frightened and I didn't know what to do.

He was waving his arms around, then he clenched his right hand into a fist and pulled it back, punching forward so fast that his fist flew into the rear-view mirror, shattering it into pieces all over the truck. He looked at his fist while there was blood gushing down from it and lifted it again, rapidly backfisting me. I was mortified! How could this happen?

He kept wiping his blood on my clothes. He told me, "That's what you get for not picking me up."

As soon as we got home, I ran into the house and down the hall to the spare bedroom, hoping he wouldn't follow. I tried to clean up all the blood on my face and my neck. He followed me and held me down while telling me I was the problem for all of this, and to just take it and shut up. The manipulation and physical abuse continued.

That next morning, I planned for my friend to pick me up after he left for an errand. I had to get out of this situation, no matter how much I thought I loved him or that he was trying to change his life around. Starting over, to me, was the only option. I had all of my things packed and shoved it in my friend's little car. No note. No retaliation. Just gone.

I thought I was free from him after I left him that morning, but he had other plans.

The manipulation continued via social media and messaging apps on my phone. He talked about me like I was trash, tried to turn my friends against me, started rumors about me, and continued to stalk me and keep tabs on my whereabouts.

I tried to ignore it all, but the manipulative content, constant death threats, trespassing, stalking and name-calling affected my everyday life. I didn't sleep or eat much for months. I felt like I was a squirrel in the road everywhere I went. I didn't feel safe at home or anywhere. I thought either he or people he knew would see me. He would ask friends of mine or others about my whereabouts. I never knew if someone was reporting to him.

He even trespassed at my home one day.

He started by pounding on my front cottage windows. The banging on the glass had me frightened he might break it. I didn't answer. It got quiet for a moment, but before I could settle, he started banging on my bedroom windows. He climbed into my backyard! I was inside the house and I fell to my knees while on the phone with a friend of mine, who was listening to everything my ex was saying and doing. My friend couldn't believe what he was hearing, for nobody ever saw this side of that man.

I finally felt like his truth had been revealed to someone. That maybe my story could finally be heard and believed! He spent so much time trying to cover himself up or kissing ass that people wouldn't believe me. My friend made me feel like I had someone I could trust by calming me down and letting me know he was there for me. It was a silver lining in the midst of feeling like my world had shattered.

Between the manipulation, rumors, and his lies about me, I lost many people from my life who had previously been my friends or at least I thought they were. I didn't know who to trust. He made me believe everyone was against me, and anything I tried to do, he'd find me. There were hundreds of texts and voicemails sent from multiple numbers, finding me on social media, stalking me at restaurants, following me home, and more. All fell into the trap of fear.

You're probably asking why I never got a restraining order or changed my phone number. Two pivotal things which could have changed the course for me, but hindsight is 20/20. I don't know how to explain what it feels like to just survive. No goals were being attained; I couldn't even think about tomorrow or the future. This whole thing affected my finances, my friendships, and any connections I had to my health. Really all the foundational pieces of success. I felt stripped of everything. I was stuck in survival mode. I couldn't move.

There is a way to navigate through these circumstances. We gain tools through our experiences in life, from childhood and every day until we have served our time here. These tools are fundamental on our journey. They help us to dust ourselves off when faced with adversity, just by reaching for them. They help smooth out the edges of once sharp stabs to our hearts and souls.

I thank my dad for being a pillar of strength throughout my childhood, showing me what it's like to treat all humans and my mother, whom he adores even more today. I always remember the words he'd tell me before I'd close the car door at school, "Do something good for someone today, just because it feels good."

No matter where we come from and the families we were raised by, we all have a voice and choices to make. Every person's voice counts. If something doesn't work, if you don't feel comfortable and know something is not right, make a change. That's the choice. Trust the voice inside telling you what is best for you. Listen to it.
I choose to keep working on myself everyday and to do something good for someone as the opportunity arises. I choose not to carry around the baggage that would be so easy to carry around from trauma and experiences in life. I choose to make myself softer in the face of hardship. To

be kinder and gentler. But also to be stronger knowing I got myself out of something which was toxic. Those experiences don't define me and judgment can't either. No matter what people think, say, or do, I will continue to move forward with my truth and my story every day.

It has also taught me to look at the people surrounding someone who is toxic. So many of us look the other way when presented with taboo or difficult topics. Let's change it around. Who are we spending our time with? Let's really take a look at ourselves, and what we are and are not okay with. It's time to look inside and at the reflections of light and dark which we share in relationships around us. It helps us become a little more aware of our own limitations and boundaries, in turn creating healthier relationships. Stand for something!

Being a part of this book has been one of many things to stand for while writing side by side with others whose voices are finally being heard!

Moving Forward
I still live in California. I love this quaint country town I'm in. It's so friendly and I have a wonderful group of friends and a different boyfriend, who celebrated my birthday with me on Christmas this year. This relationship is different and much better than what I had with my abuser. I'm working full-time and currently live on a big piece of property with goats and chickens, and what I love to call my secret garden. There are many entryways into the garden, fully covered in jasmine vines which produce wonderful smells in and around my home. There are olive trees, pomegranate trees, apple trees, lavender and roses, all kinds of squash, green beans and little garden beds of strawberries.

We recently had a major fire move through our county. Thousands of people were displaced and lost their homes. I wanted to help somehow, so I opened up my home to the fire victims to pick up belongings ranging from clothes and shoes to kitchen supplies to a bed and a TV. I felt like it was a good time to downsize. I had families of four group-hugging me while they laughed with tears to have at least something after some losing photographs and family heirlooms.

I feel full of love and life, and will continue to give back all that I can.

When I saw this project being put together it just felt serendipitous, because I am on a healing path. I am not pointing fingers or playing some sort of blame game. I wrote this to open people's eyes to the possibility of listening to our own voices and trusting ourselves enough to start the process of throwing out the things which are no longing serving us.

We are waking up and changing paradigms. I'm honored to be a part of this, where others are sharing their once-kept-secret stories. I want us to choose to do something with our united voices, stand for something, and recreate ourselves in the face of adversity. It allows everyone to heal. I hope we all find love in our hearts to continue down this road of walking together. I mean, we are ONE after all. And LOVE IS THE ANSWER.

The most important choice in life that I have is my attitude.

"Attitude is 10 percent what happens to me and 90 percent how I react to it." - Charles Swindoll

Angela Davis — Davis is an American civil rights and political activist, author, and academic. She was seen as a radical in the 1960s and once led the Communist Party USA, which had close ties to the Black Panther Party of the Civil Rights Movement. She was a professor emerita at UC Santa Cruz in the History of Consciousness department, then became the director of the university's Feminist Studies department. Davis has lectured and written several books. Her primary focus has been race, inequality, justice and feminism. She was an honorary co-chair of the 2017 Women's March on Washington and she spoke at the event.

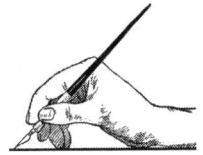

Ryan, 35, Massachusetts, USA

In the new era of #metoo, many are being forced out of #notme. Every day on the news we hear about another famous, powerful person being accused of sexual misconduct. The media is spending hours upon hours a day covering the politicians, the news anchors, the media moguls and their accusers' stories. While the Silence Breaker's movement is powerful and can make real positive changes, it also can have a negative impact and is being covered in a very irresponsible way.

At the age of 35, I am now being forced to face my own rape, which took place when I was 14, because I was living in the "not me" bubble.

At the age of 14, growing up in a conservative family in an upscale neighborhood, and attending a private Catholic school, reporting sexual assault was never an option. The questions were: what will people think of me, will people believe me, did I say no, will the neighbors still talk to my parents, will my parents still love me?

So, at the age of 14, not mature enough to process anything which happened physically, mentally, or emotionally, I made the decision to lock it away. Never to speak of it again.

What isn't discussed are the side effects of this "not me" bubble. I panic when going into confined places, I flinch if a stranger touches me, I still to this day look to see if I will see his face in the crowd. I can't listen to the song that was blasting during the assault so no one would hear me. For years, friends and family would question me about these quirks of mine and the bubble would push the words "I was raped" deeper down so they wouldn't bubble up.

With the #metoo phenomenon came the question of: Why did they wait so long? Why now?

But the media, instead of having rape counselors, survivors, or psychiatrists on their shows to answer these questions, are replying with opinions and "I don't know."

If we are going to have this conversation and make serious changes, we have the responsibility to answer these questions with experts and facts so that 14-year-old me isn't worrying about not being believed.

If we want to break the silence, we need to educate people on why the victims stayed silent for so long.

If we are going to talk about sexual violence on TV all day everyday, it is irresponsible not to promote support and resources for those of us whose "not me" bubble is being popped into the reality of #metoo.

To all you of who are thinking "not me," I see you, I hear you, I believe you, I stand with you, I speak for you.

Anita Hill – You may know her name from the Clarence Thomas controversy of 1991, when she spoke out and accused the U.S. Supreme Court nominee of sexual harassment. Anita Hill is a U.S. attorney and academic, serving as a university professor of social law policy, law, and women's studies at Brandeis University. She has written several books, including "Speaking Truth to Power" and "Reimagining Equality: Stories of Gender, Race, and Finding Home." She is a proponent of women's rights and feminism and believes in the necessity of all people needing to be represented in the U.S. legal system.

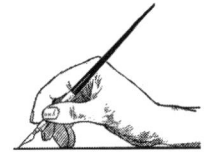

Amanda, 32, Toronto, Canada

I was working in a law firm in Toronto, Ontario. A big, prominent law firm. There's this young lawyer who expressed interest in me as soon as he met me. He emailed me. He came by to visit my desk. He asked for my number and we chatted outside of work. Then one day, he calls me into his office and tells me, "Don't close the door, I don't need a sexual harassment claim."

I have by now been in the legal industry for six to seven years and never once have I ever had any lawyer or other co-worker harass me or sexually harass me. To have him say this to me was shocking. He proceeded to tell me that I'm "the type of person to sue someone" ... meanwhile still being friendly. He would walk past my desk and ask me random questions like, "Did the old man touch you?"

I approached the managing partner of our department and told him what happened and then I was fired a few months later.

I still have not told them everything that the young lawyer said, out of fear that I would be blacklisted in this industry or labelled as being over reactive/too sensitive. I couldn't get the b*lls to tell the managing partner about the young lawyer's comment about the old man touching me, because then I would have to reveal why it bothered me so much and I haven't publicly announced yet that I am a victim of sexual assault and that the old man did touch me.

And shame on anyone who ever jokes about that, especially in the workplace and especially at a big, prominent law firm.

#disgusted #timeforachange

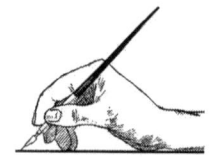

Angela, 45, California, USA

I was only 6 years old when I had my first experience with my father and his three friends, which traumatized me from that point on.

I remember it was summer time and my father was upstairs playing cards on a card table. He had three friends over and they were drinking longneck glass bottles of beer. I remember having to go to the bathroom when I was downstairs playing outside with my sister and several of our neighborhood friends. I don't really remember why I was afraid to go upstairs in my own home to go to the bathroom, but I remember the feeling of being anxious to walk up into my own place.

I remember standing at the front door looking in through the screen, asking permission to come inside. Finally he allowed me to come in, and I had a funny feeling he would try to stop me from going to the bathroom. I wasn't allowed to ever walk into the house without acknowledging him first, but on this day I had to go to the bathroom really badly. I tried to walk past my father, but he grabbed my left arm and pulled me back toward him. He stopped playing cards and his friends were laughing around the table. The next thing I knew, he let go of my left arm and I was able to go to the bathroom.

A few minutes passed by and I came out of the bathroom to go back outside and play. Once again, my father stopped me, grabbing me by the right arm. I remember facing the front door; I kept looking at the screen door hoping he would let go of me so I could run outside and play again with my sister and friends, but he never did.

He insisted on me staying and entertaining him and his friends a little bit longer. He put me on the card table and told me to lay still, but he really didn't have to ask me that, because I was already frozen in fear. The next few moments were a bit hazy, because I had blocked so much of what happened to me out of my mind for years.

Then one day it all came flooding back in, and suddenly, I was anxious and overwhelmed by the emotions all at once.

I suddenly felt like I was back on that card table being experimented on, and I felt a glass bottle between my legs. I heard my father's voice saying to me in a stern voice as he stood over me to "not move and to be still."

I remember handcuffs being put on me and my ankles being held down. That glass beer bottle with a long neck between my legs. Suddenly, I was in shock. I went to another place in my mind to stay safe and to pretend I was going to be okay while they touched my body inappropriately.

I heard his friends quietly laughing around me, and at that moment, I remember being so scared that I must have had a horrible look on my face when I looked at my father, because in the middle of what he was allowing his friends to do to me, they stopped at his request and he took me off the card table.

I'll never forget the disgust my father had on his face as he pulled me off the table and took the cuffs off my wrists, like he was disappointed in me.

Why would a father do such a thing to his own daughter and then put that pressure on her to make her think she did something wrong? Why should I have given into his sick demands? Is it not a father's duty to protect his child from harm?

My father was also sexually abused by a family member growing up, and he tried to pass that to me in the possible hopes I would keep that sickness going in the family and pass it down to my own children. But I did not.

My father was always an alcoholic and used drugs regularly. He was very egocentric and a narcissist. A legend in his own twisted mind while he fought his demons daily. His Agent Orange episodes were horrifying to live with and his nightmares became the family's nightmares. We lived in fear of him and I witnessed my mother receive countless beatings. She tried to take us and leave, but he always found us.

One day, my father didn't come back home anymore because he had gotten into an accident going the wrong way on the freeway, and almost killed himself and other drivers. I didn't see him again until I was 41 years old.

He denied any wrongdoing and even denied me the right to heal from what he had done to me so long ago. After my five-hour visit with him to find the truth, I never returned and instead released my hurt and anger with him. I took the time to write a long letter to him explaining how I would always know him as my Earthly father, but that I never wanted to see or hear from him again.

It would be another five years before he tried to reach out, but this time he wanted to use me for money. I know in my heart I did the right thing in letting him go.

He never acknowledged how he took my childhood from me, even stopping my inner child from growing for so many years. But it was time to let go and make my peace with what little I had, to find my own peaceful path. It was not easy and I was in pain, confused, and angry for what I was forced to realize, which was that I had to find my own way out of the thorned jungle he left me in. The same jungle he was forced to survive in in Vietnam, maybe even that same mental jungle he was forced to find his own way out of while his family member abused him, as well.

One thing was for certain, I was not going to let my father's sickness determine my destiny. What he did to me was very wrong and illegal. It was and still is child endangerment and abuse. He may not have answered for what he did to me all those years ago, but he burned into my head and heart what a father has no right to do to his child - take a childhood away because he could not handle his own pain. There is no excuse for it and never will be.

I became a fighter for my rights as a survivor, an advocate for both the homeless, and for abused women and children. I know firsthand what that experience has done to me. Some make it out and others are lost forever.

As time went on, I was taken advantage of by my ex-husband as well, but I know for sure "what is done in the dark, will always come to the light." I know if I had to express what I would do now, hands down I would report any incidents to the authorities immediately.

Children have a right to live, to be children, to be happy and to be loved in a healthy environment that is stable and safe for them. My mother did what she could, but she was also abused and forced to work hard for my father's dirty habits. I'm sensitive toward those I sense are abused. We are hyper-sensitive souls with a more compassionate heart, which could be seen as a weakness, but I disagree. We are more aware than we are given credit for, and if need be, we can survive more than those who were never exposed to our level of pain.

I want to help others heal and I put my heart out there so others can come to me and I can share what I know to strengthen them on their own journey to healing.

Anna North – As a writer, editor, and reporter at Vox, North specializes in covering gender-related issues. She has written or edited several publications, including Jezebel, Buzzfeed, The New York Times, and Salon. Both her fiction and non-fiction works have been published in additional publications. She has two works of fiction, "America Pacifica" and "The Life and Death of Sophie Stark," which won a literary award. As a Senior Reporter at Vox, North covers gender issues, such as reproductive rights, workplace discrimination, LGBTQ rights, masculinity, femininity, and more.

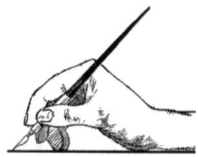

Theresa, 21, North Carolina, USA

I have a few stories, but the worst was when I worked at JC Penney right out of college. I worked with a guy in the men's clothing department. One night, it was just the two of us working. He said he was having issues with his pants and asked if I thought any of the customers would notice. I looked over and his pants were buttoned but the zipper was down - with his entire penis sticking out. I was shocked, but naively thought "Maybe he didn't know and I need to act like nothing happened so I don't embarrass him." So I told him that yes, I think someone might notice and he should get a new pair of pants, then walked away so he wouldn't feel self-conscious.

A few weeks later, I was working with a female coworker and I brought it up - talking about how I felt sorry that he had to go through something like that. She said the exact same thing happened to her and we reported him immediately.

Of course, he got fired, but another co-worker went to his church and she told the pastor. The guy got up in front of the entire congregation to admit he had a problem and that he was going to get help. But he never apologized to me or my co-worker.

Anne Dudley Bradstreet — Born in 1612, Bradstreet is touted as America's first poet, and was a pioneer in the colonies of Massachusetts. She is said to have written poetry mostly for herself and her educated family and friends. Most of her works were not discovered until nearly 200 years after her death by feminists in the 20th century. She questioned the power of male hierarchy and even God, although she was a Puritan. Her love of the spiritual and physical worlds caused creative conflict in her poetry and she could be rather humorous.

Mae, 30, Florida, USA
Fault

First

The sound of lawn mowers should never be something to be cautious of, especially to a 10-year-old girl. It meant fresh-cut grass to lay in and read, to play in, to stare into the sky and make shapes out of clouds. But childhood naivety never lasts long.

I used to walk to and from school every day, and the sound of lawn mowers was like a warning call from a watch bird perched high above me in a tree. Broward County, FL – home of Fort Lauderdale -- is like a never ending suburbia. The further west you go, the more houses become communities, and with communities come home owners' associations. The rule to have perfectly manicured lawns is strict. People who are too busy working their jobs to pay for the houses they can't afford can't take the time to do the work themselves, so they would hire lawn care companies.

I soon learned community lawn day was a day when the hair would stick up on the back of my neck. My pulse would quicken. My hearing and vision became more acute. It was the day I would mentally map a longer route home to avoid passing these communities and weigh the consequences. Risk another community having yard work done, risk being late home and hearing my mother's scolds, risk being thirsty and having to urinate so badly that I had to hide in the bushes to relieve myself? The walk was well over the two-mile limit to get bused in, but I was never zoned for the schools I attended, so I couldn't utilize that safety measure, thanks to my mother's lies to the schools.

You don't have to be cat-called to hear men staring. When the sound of the lawn mowers and weed whackers quieted, I knew what was happening. I could hear their stares first, and once one of them worked up the courage to shout, they would all start to yell.

"Hola mami! Que lo que hay?!" ("Hey girl, what's going on today?!")
"Ven paca mami!" ("Come here, girl!")
"Que haces? Porque estas caminando mas rapido?" (What are you doing? Why are you walking so fast?")

Their calls would follow me home, community after community. Week after week. I was always a small child, and am quite a petite adult, at 30, I am only 4 feet, 11 inches. I didn't speak Spanish then, but I knew their tone didn't feel welcoming. I knew that little girls shouldn't talk to strangers, especially when that stranger is a grown man.

Initially, I would offer them a small smile, a simple one – thinking it would show I meant them no harm and I just wanted to continue my walk. I soon learned it was like a welcoming sign to more taunting. I then tried ignoring them; I heard it was called giving someone the cold shoulder, so I thought I should try that. Sometimes it worked, most times it didn't. It led to walking. These men, who were never the same, started to walk toward me, calling out to me, leering at me.

One day, one of them caught up to me and grabbed my arm. I wrestled my hand free and left a man who looked stunned in my wake, and I ran home. From that day forward, I decided to never walk home near the communities which had lawn services being performed, no matter how much it extended my trip.

I never said anything, because I thought, maybe it's a language barrier? Maybe they're trying to see if I'm safe and just want to be friendly? The feeling in my belly told me I was wrong, but I didn't want to risk seeming stupid.

I should have learned to report when I felt mistreated by men. Little did I know these small advances, as harmless as they may have been, would pale in comparison to the nightmares my future would have in store for me.

Second

A few years passed, and I met my biological father. I'd begged my mother; I wanted to know who the man was who helped create me and bring me into this life. After paternity tests and court sessions, it was decided I would meet him. I was 13, and I went to Dave & Buster's with my mom to meet him. I still argue with the idea whether I would do it all differently if I could go back with the knowledge I have today. I don't think I would because it is part of what makes me who I am. But at what cost?

My father was not exceptionally wealthy, but as upper middle class, was a rung my mother had no hopes of reaching any time soon. He bought me nice things, he showered me with love and kindness, and I thought I had it all. I thought, "Finally. This is what having two parents is supposed to be like."

Then the nightmare began.

I was 14, and he asked for my help. He came and picked me up and brought me to his house.

"Mae, my business isn't doing too well, and I want to open a side business. Internet pornography is really getting big, and I want to try my hand at it. I just need some models. We don't have to have vaginal sex, but if you let me take pictures of your body in sexy undergarments, I'll buy you something nice."

What could I say? Risk saying no and losing my dad? Of course, I said yes; I finally had what I had been wanting for so many years. I let him take photos of me washing my body in the shower, of me laying on a bed, on my knees pressing my breasts together, and he promised that my face would never be in them. And I got my gifts. I didn't understand they were gifts to keep me quiet, not as thanks or out of love.

The requests became more sexual. Videos of me performing oral sex on my father, wiping his ejaculation over my nipples. He taught me the way a man likes to be pleasured. He taught me what to do with my tongue, my hands, and how much pressure to apply. I didn't realize those things couldn't show up in videos, how tight my hand was, or what my tongue was doing inside of my mouth. I had to make it look real. I had to help my dad.

Finally, when I was 16, I made him stop. I said I didn't want to do it anymore. He started to guilt me, but I threatened to tell. I told him he would have to find another model. He finally agreed, but the gifts stopped coming. His visits slowed, but he was still around. I still had a dad.

A few years later he would overhear my mother screaming at me over the phone that I had confided in my aunts, and he would abandon me in a Taco Bell parking lot, never to be heard from again. My mother's words, "Why are you telling your aunts your father is molesting you?" are forever seared into my brain.

Third

That same year, I met a boy online. I knew the dangers of online dating, but we had mutual Myspace friends whom I knew in person and who said he was a nice guy. That boy was 18 at the time and would soon join the list of names and faces I will never forget.

He came over to my house one day while my mother wasn't home, and we were hanging out. I was attracted to this boy, but all I wanted to do was maybe kiss, nothing more. We eventually ended up kissing, which led to making out, which somehow led to me on my back on my bedroom floor asking for him to stop. I begged him to stop. My closet was one of those shallow closets but with three floor-to-ceiling glass mirrors on a sliding track.

I remember how it felt as the tracks on the floor dug into my shoulders, as I felt my skin on my neck and back getting rug burn. He was forcing himself into me and was having such a difficult time that I just kept getting pushed back. He pushed and scooted himself until the top of my head hit the wall inside the closet. Until the tracks were pressing themselves into my lower back and buttocks. I was crying, knowing I was no longer a virgin, and that he had taken something from me.

He finished and went downstairs while I got dressed, silently crying to

myself. I wiped my tears, and not wanting him to think I was stupid or lame, I went downstairs and made him a plate of food.
I made him a plate of food.

I am sickened by that thought. This boy saw nothing wrong with what he did and the culture to not seem lame, stupid, or uncool made me think I should continue to treat him as a guest, even after what he did. He finished his plate and left, never to return. I didn't report him because I thought to myself, "What would the police say? I did invite him over, after all. Besides, if mom finds out, she'll beat me."

A week later, I messaged him thinking I was pregnant. "You're just paranoid. You're not pregnant." And then he blocked me. Thankfully, I wasn't pregnant, but I realized that he was only interested in me for the sex. For the notch on his belt.

Fourth

When I was 19, I was the other woman. I had moved away from the tyrannical grip of my mother to a small college town in north central Florida. Gainesville, home of the Florida Gators. My years of abuse had caught up to me and I was sexually promiscuous, not truly caring about myself or my partners. I worked and went to school, and at night, I drank.

I was dating a guy who kept promising to leave his fiancée. When I finally had enough, I broke things off and demanded my apartment key back. He said he would give it to me in a few days. Pacified, I went about my day and skipped an after-work party I knew he would be at.

I woke up in the middle of the night to banging on my door. He demanded I let him in. When I refused, he unlocked the door with his key, but the door caught on the chain lock. He kept kicking and kicking until finally, the chain gave. He was drunk and demanding that I take him back. I refused and threatened to call the police. The last thing I remembered was him punching me. I woke up in my bed with him on top of me, thrusting himself into me over and over. I started to struggle, but when I tried to move my arms my head began to swim. I remember looking out my bedroom window, waiting for him to finish.

When he did, he rolled over and fell asleep. I knew I was ovulating and I knew, deep down, I was going to get pregnant. I called him a few weeks later and told him I had scheduled an abortion and wanted him to pay for half of it. He was furious, but when I threatened to call the police and have him deported back to Guatemala, he handed over the money. He called me a baby killer.

My fetus was 8 weeks, 2 days old.

I didn't report him because his family depended on the money he was sending back home, and I felt guilty about what would happen to them should he be deported.

I left Gainesville shortly after that and went back home to South Florida. My mother's house was not exactly warm and welcoming, but I wasn't around him anymore. After that, I went into relationships where I was either controlled or mentally and emotionally abused. I never let another man put his hands on me in a physically abusive way, but I felt strong enough to endure the verbal abuse. I was very wrong.

I am now a 30-year-old woman, ironically, back living in Gainesville, Florida, again. I have forgiven all of the transgressions of the men who have hurt me. I have realized I cannot let this anger fester inside of me. I am a nurse now, and I tell women to always report, as I wish I had in the past. I now realize that their behavior creates consequences they and their families must endure. It is not my fault.

It. Is. Not. My. Fault.

Artemisia Gentileschi – 1593-1653. Gentileschi was the daughter of Italian painter Orazio, who taught her the skill from an early age. She only learned to read and write when she was an adult, but produced several works of art much earlier. Another painter, Agostino Tassi, raped Gentileschi and he was subsequently prosecuted. Although Tassi was convicted, Artemisia received unwanted publicity which ruined her reputation. Tassi was sued by Orazio for injury and damages, and the transcripts still exist today. Gentileschi's painting reflects a cathartic expression of rage and violation as a result of the pain and shame of such public scrutiny of her rape. She portrays strong women as her subjects in her work. "Judith Beheading Holofernes," for example, shows the biblical character committing the act of murder as vengeance.

Anna, 20, Russia

Here is my story about sexual harassment from bullies with whom I studied. My name is Anna. I am a 20-year-old Kazakh girl, a virgin, and I have been living in Russia for 12 years.

I was studying at cram school at my town, Apatity. In 2013, a guy who was unfamiliar to me started to walk around me and follow me, and I felt like he might want to rape me, and I was scared of his actions and the way he followed me.

In 2014, a man I did not know at all started demanding that I perform fellatio on him in a rude manner. I was 17 and I just started to crying because I was afraid that he would force and rape me, and because he sounded very offensive to me.

In 2015, some bullies started to call me "whore," "bitch," and more for no reason. They actually said and promised to rape me every day, and they told me I should become a porn actress. One of them wanted to take off his pants in front of me during a history lesson and he wanted me to perform fellatio on him.

Now I'm not afraid to tell this story about sexual harassments. I was really sexually harassed by these guys.

Asia Argento - Argento is an Italian actress, singer, model, activist, and director. Born the daughter of Italian film director, producer, and screenwriter, Dario Argento, she began acting at age 9. She claims to not have a very close relationship with her father and alleged in a 2017 New Yorker article by writer Ronan Farrow that she had been sexually assaulted by Harvey Weinstein in the 1990s and had then had multiple consensual sexual relations with him over the course of the next 5 years. She was criticized for expressing her #metoo story by her home country of Italy and moved to Germany to escape the culture of "victim blaming" there.

Julia Freifeld – #MeToo Original Song

Original song by Julia Freifeld
Music by Daniel Lomayesva

Music and video found here: https://youtu.be/w9i1EjCnCaI
Printed and published with permission from the artist.

Lyrics:
I'm tired
I'm tired of waiting
I've slowly been losing my patience
I'd like to inspire some change
We're trying
We're trying to find our voice,
Hoping that someone will listen and hear us so children don't have the same fate
We're fighting
We're fighting for something worth justice
We're fighting for a plague upon us
A plague that affects everyone I know

Me too
Me too
I would like to change this too
I would like to feel as though we're safe
Me too
Me too
I would like to see this through
We have power in the mess we've made
So come on keep fighting
We're fighting for something worth justice

We're fighting for a plague upon us so children don't have the same fate
We're trying
We're trying to change the world we know
A world that can make us feel so small
A world that can turn its back on survivors

Me too
Me too
I would like to change this too
I would like to feel as though we're safe
Stand tall
Stand tall
I was once made very small
We won't let the future know our pain

Me too
Me too
I would like to see this through
We have power in the mess we've made
So come on keep fighting

Barbara Walters — Walters was the first female co-host of a news show (although she earned only half that of her male co-workers) and she also became the first female co-anchor of an evening news broadcast for ABC News. From the 1970s through now, Walters paved the way not only for women in journalism, but for women in the entire workforce.

B, 30, Arizona, USA

My story happened when I was 16. My father lived abroad, and as a bored teenager, my dad set me up with a family friend of theirs, a local celebrity who was known for his social life. I was dying to do anything but stay home, so they figured he would be able to help get me out of the house a bit. He was 42.

He took me to a restaurant where he knew the owner. He ordered wine and dinner. I drank and ate. And drank more of the wine he kept giving me. He insisted that I drink it. Not wanting to offend a parent's friend, I did as I was told.

When it was time to leave, we were both intoxicated, but he chose to drive anyway. He drove us to the top of a nearby mountain. He pulled off to the side of the road and told me to get out of the car. I knew something was wrong. The phone I had was dead. I had no way of calling for help.

I told him I wanted to go home. He shouted for me to get out. I got out. He led me to a gate in the woods where he told me he owned the property.

I walked through the gate and down the path. Trembling now and feeling sober despite the amount of wine I had consumed, I remember thinking to myself as I continued to walk "this could be it for me. They'll never find my body. I'm in a foreign country. If I run now, he will catch me." Terrified doesn't begin to describe it.

As we walked down in the "woods" he owned, he began to take off his clothes. He left a trail of them in front of me as he became naked. He showed me a mattress on top of a wooden platform that looked like a camping bedroom. He told me women beg to come here.

He bathed naked in the stream nearby and asked me to watch him. It was pitch black beyond the one light he brought with us.

I sat on a picnic table near the steam and did as I was told. When he was done bathing himself, he asked if he could sit at the table with me. Scared, I said yes. He then asked if he could kiss me and touch me. I said no. He did it anyway.

He reached down my shirt and kissed from my hand up my arm. I started crying.

I told him I wanted to go home. He told me I had been "giving him signals" all night long and that I wanted him. I told him I didn't.

I got up and started walking toward the car. Shouting that I was done and wanted to go home. After 20 minutes of coaxing, he agreed to take me home.

When I got to my condo, he put his hand down my shirt one last time and kissed me. I did not kiss him back. I did not move his hand. I just sat there. Frozen.

As soon as he pulled away, I fell apart. He was a trusted family friend. Someone with a public reputation. No one would believe me. To this day, I'm not sure anyone does.

 *Bell Hooks* - *This American author was known for her social activism which was often mirrored through her writing of oppression, women's rights, and race. Some of Hooks' most notable works include "Ain't I A Woman? Black Women and Feminism" and "The Feminist Theory," in which she declared, "Feminism is a movement to end sexism, sexist exploitation and oppression."*

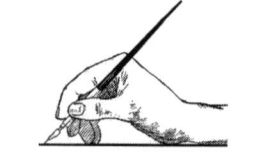

Josh, 43, California, USA

#METOO
"Thanks… to those who ensured there was light,
even when all seemed so dark. #MeToo"
@JustJoshLamont, Oct 15, 2017

Most of what I know about my early childhood comes not from my own memory, but the telling and embellished retelling of stories from my parents and doting grandparents. Classics include me being "totally bilingual" in preschool, eating nothing but peas and carrots for six months, and the infamous family intervention on my fourth birthday to address a pacifier addiction (my grandfather's version ends with me walking around the house, gathering up the 100-plus pacifiers I had apparently hidden, including several buried in the backyard).

Since none of these storytellers saw it for themselves, I don't know when precisely I was first molested by (XX). I don't remember the specific day when he first touched me sexually, or forced me to do the same. But I know it happened and I know it went on for the better part of my childhood. For better or worse, I remember far more than I don't.

Around first grade, XX (now 16) called it our "bonding time," and to me, it was a part of life. I didn't like it, but I also didn't like cauliflower or gym class – and like these, I thought bonding time was also mandatory.

From my parents, I know that XX first came into my life when he was a student at a rural Northern California school where my dad was his teacher, mom was the school's cook and tutor, and I was an adorable 2-year-old who apparently roamed freely like I ran the place (as the assuredly embellished story goes).

When the school was forced to close, XX's parents made it clear their

13-year-old son was not welcome and "better off living on the streets." My young parents, barely 10 years older than XX, suggested he stay with us "for a while" in San Diego, where my parents met as teenagers, and I was born, and we would live in the same house together until I left for college.

For the next seven years, I shared a bedroom with XX, now introduced as "my foster brother," who physically, mentally and sexually abused me almost nightly, until I was 11 and he left our house to enlist in the Marine Corps. Those last months we shared a room were the worst, as he became more aggressive and forceful, often ejaculating on (or many times in) my body. I hadn't yet hit puberty, but still XX would painfully attempt to "arouse" me, becoming angry and more abusive when my body would not respond as he wanted.

When he left for the Marines, I thought the nightmare was over. I understood at this point that our "bonding time" was NOT normal, but I never for a moment considered telling anyone, my parents especially. It was over, so why bother? And besides, who would benefit knowing?

XX, to my dismay, remained a presence for holidays and long breaks, often bringing girlfriends and others over to meet my parents "and his nerdy kid brother." I dreaded every visit, and was often scolded for not showing him affection and seemingly (and truthfully) not accepting him as part of our family. My dread turned to resentment, anger and depression, all hidden by the character of myself I created as the book-smart extrovert, voted *Most Likely to Succeed* by my classmates.

After high school, the character readied for a new chapter, far from home.

From an early age, when boys were talking about girls they liked, I was thinking about them. Being gay was not something talked about the way it is today, even as my parents' core group of friends was predominantly gay men and a lesbian couple. While I admired and respected gay people, I assumed XX somehow "made me gay," which made me hate him more.

Despite my preference for men, my first kiss and later my first consensual sexual experience were with a woman, soon after orientation at Cornell. I met Dominique my first day on campus and we began dating, when after one night studying together, she leaned over to kiss me. It felt good and I enjoyed it, in part because it was safe and also because it meant an end to studying for chemistry class, which I enjoyed about as much as gym class and cauliflower.

Over the next few months, while my relationship with Dominique blossomed, at night I began having increasingly violent nightmares, all various versions on the same story: XX chasing me with some kind of weapon – the gun dream, the rope dream, the knife dream. The dreams and my terror became more intense as winter break approached, knowing tradition meant XX would be seated across from me at Christmas dinner.

Adding anger to my anxiety, my parents had called one day near the end of first semester with a request. I hadn't seriously considered going to a private university, given the expense, until Cornell offered me an almost full-scholarship, save for a $2,000 annual family contribution. Accepting what seemed too good to be true, my parents offered to cover the $2,000, and I committed to working part-time and paying for my own travel home for breaks and personal expenses. With Christmas approaching, mom wanted to change the plan, asking me to work a bit more or get a loan so my parents could instead use their $2,000 commitment to help XX buy a new car (If I could pitch-in for the car, even better!).

I hung up the phone and lost it. I was alone with Dominique who knew instantly something was wrong. I began shaking uncontrollably, unable to speak and my vision becoming blurred. In the midst of this panic attack, I was completely reliant on Dominique's calming, safe arms, and once I settled down, she became the first person I ever told about growing up, sharing a room with XX.

Today, Dominique and I still keep in touch now and again, randomly running into each other not long after 9/11 in a London coffee shop. We had years before ended our relationship, as her friends were getting marriage proposals and I was secretly subscribing to gay magazines. We went several years without speaking, and aren't especially close now, but it was – and is – always good to connect, and at times, as I will now, thank her for being so many firsts for me, especially the first person to hear that I was molested by XX.

I went home for Christmas break freshman year, supported by Dominique and a campus therapist, ready to tell my parents about XX and my childhood of abuse. I arranged to be home before him, telling mom and dad there was something private I needed to discuss. Dad thought it was about the car money for XX, and mom (years later) admitted she thought I was going to come out of the closet, revealing Dominique to be a man. Neither were prepared for what I had to share with them.

Telling my parents was a catharsis beyond my expectations. As I finished answering their questions, I actually smiled and felt a release of pain and rush of euphoria I had never known.

I was also prepared for my parents to be upset, with a local therapist at the ready to meet with all of us that very day. Still, the pain they were feeling that moment was unmistakable – and my own mind started racing with thoughts of what it must be like to feel my pain experienced over many years, cumulatively dropped on them all at once.

My dad, an amiable, humble special ed teacher whom I had never seen get emotional was so overcome with tears and rage, the post he was leaning on began to visibly shake as he forcefully pounded against it in silent pain. Mom, through the expressions on her face seemingly cycled through all seven stages of grief at once, darting from denial to anger, bargaining and a then reluctant acceptance, without saying a word.

They were now victims of my trauma and in the days and months to follow, with the help of a therapist, our love for each other, and the immediate and complete excision of XX from our lives, it brought us closer than ever.

As I experienced seeing so many #MeToo stories recently, I thought of my own. My initial thoughts were not around my childhood, but an experience coming later as an adult.

At 20, I was comfortably living my truth as a gay man, wrapping up a term as a White House intern (down the hall from fellow interns Monica Lewinsky and Huma Abedin) and excited about life ahead. At night I worked in a gay coffeehouse across the street from a Cornell-owned apartment building, where I lived. I was dating here and there, and making fast friends working at the coffeehouse, particularly from the crowds who came in nightly after the gay bars around closed.

I was having the time of my life. Until I wasn't.

On August 18, 1995, I was locking up the coffeehouse doors around 4 a.m., when a friend and another man I did not know walked over, clearly intoxicated (on what I didn't know). I knew one of the men, José, quite well – spending time with him and his boyfriend, who seemed to be living the ideal life of two men in love, building a life together.

I offered to get José and his friend a taxi, making small talk until I could safely put them both into the car. The flirtatious stranger convinced me to join them to "make sure they got there," which I foolishly fell for. An hour later, the stranger was forcefully holding me down, my face squashed into the pillows of the bed by the weight of his knees on the back of my neck and head, while José raped me. The two traded roles, as my body instinctively resisted by simply falling limp as I had for so many years with XX in our shared bedroom.

As José and the stranger moved their party to another room in the house, I remained still and silent, covered in a mix of my own blood and their semen. When the men who raped me eventually crashed in another room, I got dressed and quietly walked out the front door and started the 45-minute walk home.

As when I was a child, I had no intention of telling anyone.

A few years later, my parents got a fresh start with a surprise move to Hawaii for their 30th anniversary. I was again living as the character I created in grade school, full of life and friends, taking New York by storm, Ivy League degree in hand, personally fulfilled by the professional experiences which would take me around the world, working with inspiring and high-profile boldface names, eventually leading to a return to the White House where I once interned, this time as an appointee of President Barack Obama.

I have been blessed with many extraordinary experiences, but fulfillment and happiness have been elusive more often than not. Now 43, while I have been in and out of relationships with a number of great men, my longest romantic relationship is the year-and-a-half I spent with Dominique 25 years ago, the one and only woman I've ever dated. I thought I would be a dad myself by now, even if on my own, but as my friends and peers have started their families, old fears have effectively extinguished my dreams. Even with XX a distant memory and long out of my life, I cannot imagine bringing a child into the world who might experience a sexual trauma at the hands of a monster like him, José or some nameless drunk. I don't believe I have the strength to experience what I saw in my parents' eyes the day I told them about XX.

Over the years, my parents and I became less close at times, with periods of stress, mistrust, and resentment; our shared connection to XX almost always playing a part in our pain and depression, each of us self-medicating in our own way with food, drugs, and alcohol.

In 2013, my mom passed away at 59 from brain cancer. I left the White House to be with her and my dad for the last few months of her life. We were close again and it was a beautiful time together. Mom opened up about the pain she could never fully let go of for inviting XX into our lives, and I shared my own resentments for the sacrifices I perceived she'd made, too often putting others, including XX, before Dad, me and herself. Holding her hand, we asked each other for forgiveness.

Today, the character known as the kid voted Most Likely To Succeed, who went from the Ivy League to the White House (twice), is once again back working with bold-faced names making the world a better place, but primarily from home so that I can also care for Dad as he fights the good fight against Parkinson's.

My mom wrote a short poem as a teenager including the line, "to have never loved is to have been a character in a play; and never really lived. At all."

My character continues to need help, make mistakes and experience pain. Yet I do not regret a single day, choice or experience I have had in my life

-- not even my time with XX or José. All of the experiences of my life inform who I am today, and I do not want to be anyone other than who I am, even as I hope the character I play is eventually revealed to be the good, fulfilled, happy and genuine man I aspire to be.

#MeToo

Betty Friedan - *This American writer and activist penned "The Feminine Mystique" in 1963, which is often credited for sparking the second wave of feminism that swept through the 60s and 70s. Friedan spent her life working to establish women's equality, helping to establish the National Women's Political Caucus, as well as organizing the Women's Strike For Equality in 1970, which popularized the feminist movement throughout America. "No woman gets an orgasm from shining the kitchen floor," she is quoted as saying.*

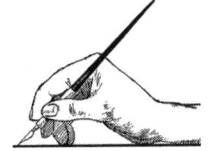

Mandy, 32, Florida, USA

I was 13 and naive. I feel like that is the consensus of most people of all 13-year-olds. I guess I proved them right.

I had a friend who invited me to her birthday party. That was where I met him. He seemed nice, and he must have been to be friends with my friend. She was a kind soul, so I assumed the same for her other friends. I assumed wrong.

He was older, yes. 16 to my 13, and he seemed to take a liking to me at the party. He invited me to a movie later and I agreed, so we exchanged numbers. Later, he called, and my parents allowed him to take me out, unaware of his age and lack of parental involvement.

He took me on a few dates before taking me to a concert, Metallica to be exact. It was a great concert at the beginning. But halfway through the concert he ran into a group of his friends and he changed.

He dragged me into a corner with his friends. My back to the wall, literally.

He kissed me roughly and grabbed hold of my hair. When he pulled away, he forced me to my knees. I tried to pull away, but a friend of his grabbed my arms, forcing them behind my back. He let go of my hair and unzipped himself.

"I've waited long enough." That was all he said as he grabbed my hair once again and pushed me toward his member.

I kept my mouth closed until the boy holding my arms called another friend over and he grabbed one of my arms while he wrapped his around my neck. That forced me to gasp out to try to breathe. It was then that he forced his dick into my mouth with the threat of injury if I bit him.
I remember the tears in my eyes and me struggling to breathe through the

other guys grip around my neck. I remember him grunting as he forcibly rammed himself into my mouth; it felt like it was going to go straight through the back of my head. Tears streamed down my face and then a horrible taste went down my throat. He pulled out and put himself away. Then he congratulated me on a job well done, and looked forward to the next time, stating how his friends should give it a try.

The friend with his arm around my neck laughed as he let go of my one arm he was still holding and grabbed me below the belt. Then he licked up my cheek. "I look forward to it," he said as he let go of me. The other boy pushed me down on the ground. He told them not there and pulled me up, acting all sweet and innocent.

He took me home and told me if I told anyone that his father, a police officer, would arrest me and I would sit in a jail cell. Being 13, I believed him and never uttered a word. He tried to call me again and I told my parents I didn't want anything to do with him anymore. I was done, and he was mean, and left it at that. He came to the house once and I hid in my room as my father told him I didn't want to see him again and to leave.

That was the last time I saw him, but he did call one more time; he just said to remember I will know if you tell.

I never did. Until now.

Brigitte Macron -Becoming France's First Lady in 2016, Brigitte Macron breaks a lot of molds society has placed upon women. She is 64 years to President Emmanuel Macron's 40, and is seen as a powerful sounding board for issues on which she knows well: education, culture, and women's rights. She encourages her husband to include proposals for smaller classes for students in disadvantaged areas, for instance. She also helps to advance women in politics in France, as President Macron has pledged that half the candidates his party's fields will be women, with many appointed to his cabinet, as well.

Rachael C., 39, Gold Coast, Australia

Healing the Shame of Sexual Abuse

It's taken me awhile to find the right words around this movement. To me, this is not just a social awareness campaign, it's an active part of my healing. And I hope it is for many men and women around the world who are finding the courage and vulnerability to add their voices.

My story began when I was 7 years old. In my small fragile mind I had no idea how to deal with what happened to me. What I now understand is that my nervous system did not go into fight or flight; however, it did freeze. I did not know what to do with this energy, and subsequently my survival instincts kicked in and blocked the whole experience from my memory. A lot of normal and wonderful childhood memories also got buried within that mechanism which instinctively knew I did not have the capacity to deal with it at that time.

Later, at 14 years old, I was in a drama class at school. It was the afternoon session and we were making masks from plaster of paris for our Greek drama module. I had Vaseline smeared all over my face and my partner was laying the plaster over my face gently, when the teacher started playing some quiet meditation music. As the process continued I found myself drifting into a meditative space. I was very calm and peaceful, my eyes closed and secured behind the plaster, and I had nowhere to run, no exit route.

In the middle of that void, a movie screen appeared in front of me and three still images flashed on the screen. This was the moment that changed my world.

Those images were triggers for the memories to be uncovered in my conscious mind. I remembered two different boys, one five years older than me, one 10 years older, and both of them were friends of my two brothers (Sam, 12, and Michael 17, at the time of the first incident).

One boy lived around the corner from our childhood home where I would remain living until I was 19. That was literally "close to home." Let's call him Peter. The other one was a friend of my other brother and was a regular visitor to our house -- Jack.

The memories which leaked into my awareness were mainly pertaining to Peter. While I only had those three images appear to me, the knowing behind them were that the sexual molestation I had been subjected to from Peter had gone on for over a year while Jack was a one-off encounter. None of these experiences were something that should ever have happened to a 7 year old girl. Peter was 10 years my senior, and at 17 years of age, he had somehow arranged to get me alone with him in our laundry. Not only was I touched inappropriately, I was coaxed to touch him inappropriately. It went on for at least a year, every chance he had to get me alone -- he would.

Once the mask was off my face and I was able to get away from the class full of people who were totally oblivious to what had happened in my inner world, I ran as fast as I could. I left school, I cried all the way home and once I was in the safety of my room behind the closed door of an empty house, I howled like a banshee. I recovered myself enough by the time my mum and dad got home from work. I made it through dinner with the family and after my parents left for a meeting for the night, I was again alone with my pain.

Then the doorbell rang. I went to answer the door and my breath caught in my throat as I saw Jack standing on the front steps. I inched the door ajar and he said "Hi, is Sam home? Oh my god, you must be little Rach, all grown up!" I abruptly told Jack "Sam isn't home, I'll let him know you stopped by." I slammed the door shut and ran for the safety of my room. I looked up toward the heavens and cried, "Is this some kind of sick joke, God? What the f*ck was that?!"

I was still crying when Sam returned home from work. Now 19 years old and still my closest friend, he knew I was not in a good place. I opened up to him about what had happened both at school and while at home alone that night. He supported me so lovingly, he allowed me to get it out, to put into words the experience I remembered, vague as it was. He hugged me and reassured me I was safe and gently told me what I knew but did not want to face: "You really should tell Mum & Dad, Rach; you will need their support to heal this."

I'm unsure of how much time passed before I did tell my mum. Her heart broke, of course, and as we worked through it, she told me I needed to tell my dad. When I finally worked up enough courage to face my father and share what had unfolded, he brushed it off as kids playing doctors and nurses, and went on working in the yard. It was a Saturday afternoon, and while I knew he loved me, I knew he had not really heard me. Maybe he didn't want to face the truth either. Maybe he just didn't have the head space to stop what he was doing and be present with me.

That exchange broke me a little more, it set up the story that I then continued to gather evidence of for over a decade of how I was unworthy of being heard or truly listened to. Mum had seen me run once more to my room in tears and came to find out what had happened. She gently pushed me back out the door to go and tell Dad he needed to listen, to hear me and understand what I was saying. Bless her, I am so glad she did, because it was so important that everyone in the family know the truth of the matter. I needed their support.

As my dear father finally realised it was serious and sat to really hear me, I felt his anger rise. He wanted to get the cricket bats out, gather my brothers, and march around to Peter's house and gain some revenge, dole out some payback. In my heart, I was relieved someone cared enough to want to inflict pain on this person, yet I stopped him. I told him this was my job. I had to face my abuser and deal with it in my way. I'm not sure how Dad sat back down, but I remember his assurance that he would be there for me when I returned.

I knew there was no point in putting myself or my family through the ordeal of going to the police. My young mind understood enough of the patriarchal society I grew up in to know it would be a case of he said-she said, and as so many years had passed I would probably be the one to suffer most through that. So, I knew it was up to me and me alone.

I walked up the road, around the corner, crossed the street and knocked on the door. Peter answered the knock and I asked to speak to him in the yard. I have no idea where I got the courage or the words that day. Yet through my tears I straightened my back, looked him squarely in the eye and said, "I remember what you did to me. It wasn't right or okay. I'm angry at you and you owe me and my family one big fat apology."

Peter was clearly taken aback and after a moment he said in reply, "I didn't know it was wrong, it happened to me when I was young." No sorry, no acknowledgement of the pain I was feeling, just self-pity and justification was all he gave me.

I shot straight back at him, "Just because it happened to me, I am never going to turn around and hurt another small child, that's not how it works." I felt the flush of rage hit my face and I turned and walked away.

For many years, I denied the shame I felt. I pushed it away. I numbed it away and refused to look, to allow it a voice. I finally started sharing with those closest to me. My best friends and my family all supported me wonderfully to talk through it.

What I didn't understand back then was that there are many layers to uncover and it can't all be done in a single conversation, a day, a week, or even a year. I thought that because I had shared it at the time, I was healed, that I had moved passed it. I hadn't. I had simply dealt with as much as what I had the capacity to at the time.

Almost 25 years later and the health journey I have been on for the past 18 or so months has been a deeper level uncovering of pain, shame and anger, and unresolved emotions begging for light to be cast upon them. This time presented the opportunity to heal the deepest held layers of trauma.

What has also presented itself for healing is all the diversions I threw upon the original trauma unconsciously, in an effort to deny there was still work to be done. Most of those diversions compounded the shame, the fear of humiliation, the unmet guilt and denial, the self-deprecation, and spiral of negative self-talk.

I self-medicated with drugs for many years, into my 30s. Some of those addictions brought me close to the edge of losing my life and those I loved. I didn't understand why I so often found myself in relationships where my partners had stronger feelings for me than I did for them, causing me to run away and bail on them with no explanation. Or it was the other end of the scale, either suffering from unrequited love or with men who I unconsciously deemed as "safe" because they were older and didn't love me, yet they were happy to use me for sex. I felt that was all that I was good for over many years.

I never really found those feelings I craved of being truly loved and honored; those elusive feelings I now understand to be my own heart calling out for me to provide the love and honor to myself. This process has taken many years and a chronic illness for me to actually stop and uncover that what I need most is my own unconditional love of self. To forgive myself for any belief I have held which is incongruent with the fact that I am a child of the Divine who is worthy of great love, who is not broken or in need of fixing, who is not a problem, but is here for a purpose and is precious is all ways. I have been guided to find the deepest levels of forgiveness for myself, for anyone who has ever hurt me, and for the collective consciousness's deviation from the truth that we are all one.

Shame is one human emotion we all struggle to deal with, regardless of the cause of the shame. This movement gives us an opportunity to create a discourse around that dark and shadowy human emotion.

It's no coincidence that just before the #metoo's began to flood social media I came across Brene Brown's work. She is a researcher on the specific subject of shame. I listened to a powerful conversation she had with Oprah on her SuperSoul Sundays podcast, and one thing struck me deeply -- the point in her research which showed that shame cannot withstand empathy. Shame cannot survive empathy.

Think on that for a moment. For someone to show us empathy, we must first make ourselves vulnerable and share the source of our shame with another. We must discern carefully with whom we share vulnerability, especially when we are still bleeding from the pain. We must trust the person we share with will have the capacity to empathize instead of colonize, sympathize or worse, dishonor or ignore our vulnerability. The empathy my friends and family gave to me as a 14-year-old girl helped me heal as much as I could and was ready to at that time.

Again now, as I approach my 40th year, my nearest and dearest have continued to hold a space of non-judgment, deep empathy, and love for me as I have pulled up the last of those gnarled and insidious roots which had grown so deep in my psyche. For them, I am eternally grateful. I pray everyone needing that support finds a way to receive it and be healed from the pain sexual abuse and harassment can inflict.

So for those of you who are still finding the courage to share your story or simply put your #metoo in the ring, those discerning the right people or place or forum to share it with or just struggling with the base emotions an experience like this generates, I want you to know that I honor your path.

I am willing to witness you and I truly can empathize with the effects such an experience can have. I share my vulnerability from a place of empowerment and the ability to hold space for myself regardless of what someone may or may not be able to empathize with. I hold the rim of my container with a fierce love for myself and my journey, for it has made me the woman I am today. It may have taken decades of detours and roundabouts to get here and learn to love myself, and for that I'm proud of me.

I celebrate me, and I wish for each and every person walking this earth to have the privilege of meeting their own fears and pain with strength and humility because on the other side of that shitstorm is an unshakable knowing that each of us is a divine, deeply loved piece of a benevolent universe which is always working on our behalf.

I invite you today to find a deeper level of love for yourself than you have discovered. I encourage you to then find a deeper level of love for your fellow humans and get vulnerable, allow yourself to be seen (with discernment!), and allow your deepest shadows to be healed.

Find a way to forgive yourself. You deserve that forgiveness and love, regardless of what you have or haven't done. Then find forgiveness for those who have harmed you. For when we hold ill will or unforgiveness in our hearts toward others, we are only swallowing poison ourselves while expecting the other to die.

These are extraordinary times we live in. For no small reason, we now as a collective have the awareness, which grows with each person who puts his or her hand up and says "me too." I believe none of us are broken, none of us need fixing for we are the divine incarnate, we are all on our way home to the awareness that we are one, knowing we are whole and are in the process of experiencing ourselves as the god consciousness that we are!

#stoptheshame
#endthesilence

Cecile Richards - Cecile Richards hails from Waco, Texas and is an American pro-choice activist, serving as the president of the Planned Parenthood Federation of America and Planned Parenthood Action Fund since 2006. She has been a labor organizer for service workers across several states and ran union campaigns for many before she was 30 years old. She currently serves on the Ford Foundation Board, which is a global private foundation advancing human welfare. She also is one of the founders and current President of America Votes, an organization whose goals are to coordinate and promote progressive issues.

You Are Not Alone

Anonymous Twitter Story

(shared with permission)

#MeToo.

1st grade. The school principal leaned me over his lap, lifted my dress and spanked me. I cried. He pulled down my panties and rubbed my bottom. His hand moved between my legs. I remember feeling tingly and I think I peed a little on him. I was very ashamed. I suffered from anxiety and started wearing thick denim shorts under my dresses every day. I became terrified of every principal and male teacher I had after that.

I was later raped when I was 14 years old by a neighbor friend. He was in his 20s. He took me for a ride to show me his new car and gave me a drink with vodka in it, which made me fall asleep. I woke up feeling sick and he was on top of me. I started crying. I was a virgin and bled on his car seat. He was furious about the mess and took me home. He said if I told anyone he would kill me. I believed him and I never told a soul.

I now wish I had.

Chimamanda Ngozi Adichie *- Most known for her "We Should All Be Feminists" TED Talk, which was sampled on Beyoncé's self-titled album, Adichie has become a vital author in the modern day feminist movement. Some of her most prominent pieces, "Americanah," "We Should All Be Feminists," and "Dear Ijeawele, Or a Feminist Manifesto in Fifteen Suggestions," have been instrumental in advocating for women's rights and representing African culture.*

Helena, 68, Portugal

It's an old story, similar to many other people. It's being going on since mankind existed in every quarter of the globe.

Just this year, I got the courage to disclose to my family, my husband and children, what happened, and what a weight it was off my shoulders to finally say it out loud.

It is hard to explain, but I felt free.

Last year, I contacted his widow and asked her a few questions. I asked, "Were you aware that he would follow me? That he knew where I was and with whom I had been?"

She replied, "Oh, he liked the attention of young girls."

I said, "You both were educated and multilingual. He was a lieutenant colonel, a big deal." I couldn't believe her answer to me. He was the head of the four military branches in Portugal, a big shot with authority and power.

I explained how I had not initiated anything with him, ever. I simply wanted to care for their kids, as I had been hired to do, with the understanding I would still be able to go to my classes. Their three children were 11, 9, and 7 years old.

As I became aware over the next decades, and as I got older, I understood the power these types of people have over young innocent minds. I began to understand that it wasn't me.

That man tried to groom me while I was in his employ. I was there a lot, time spent in his company with the kids, and that's how he tried to get close to me. He was 47 years old and I was only 16.

I was employed there for three years, and the whole time I endured uncertainty. I constantly would be looking over my shoulder; when I was outside, he would lurk, and suddenly out of nowhere be there next to me.

It was one touch here, one word there, a praise, a compliment, and so on.

"God, keep me safe," I would say to the Virgin Mary, "If you should keep me safe until I get married one day, staying clean, the same way as when I was born."

By the grace of God and my deep beliefs, I did fall in love and get married. We had three kids. They are my legacy and what I fought for. One is an executive with Microsoft, two degrees and a Master's; my middle child has two degrees and works for the D.O.J.; my youngest is a lawyer with the United States Senate.

Back to my abuser's widow. I continued to ask her if she had realized that I was only 16 years old and if she even cared. Why would she continue to hire young girls if she had any hint at all this was going on?

All she would say was, "Oh! He has already paid his penance." Because he passed away and he had to meet his judgment.

I asked her if she ever thought he might have been a pedophile and why would she leave her husband home while she traveled overseas (from Portugal or to the Capital) for an entire week at a time.

In the end, while talking to her, she gave me the impression I was to blame. She was an enabler, though maybe not conscious of her actions. It's very typical -- blaming the kids. Back then, television was new. Nothing like now, where one can Google and search for just about anything.

As I remembered my past and became educated on these issues, I knew he groomed me under false pretenses. After three years, I was out. Do you think he stopped looking for me? At 21, I left the country, partly because I wanted to get away from him.
By then, I had met my present husband. I finally knew that my life was starting anew. In 1971, I came to the United States and the rest is history. I

mustered the courage to tell my eldest sister finally. Why I didn't feel like I could tell her sooner is the same reason why so many go decades in silence. There are people who when told will deflect or say, "Oh! It never happened to me, I was always respected."

But pedophiles don't want to respect young people's bodies or privacy. They want to conquer them for their own sick pleasure.

I am hoping my grandchildren, two beautiful little girls, will not have to worry about being abused in any way. God's angels kept my beautiful daughter safe without ever revealing my past. I managed to talk to her about the different types of good and bad in this world, but it was difficult. There is more good than bad, but we have to be vigilant and instill in their beautiful young minds that they deserve to be heard without judgment, to be believed, and that we will support them and encourage them to march on. That they matter.

That they do not need to keep a secret like mine, which might destroy one's view on life and people for decades.

If it had happened today, if that man were to be inappropriate with me, I would speak out. I would press charges and his family life and high profile position would be compromised. He was from the same era as Carlos Cruz, a famous news anchor who served prison time for basically the same crimes, though he was a lot younger than my abuser and his wife.

You may wonder why I didn't leave that job earlier. There are too many whys and what-if's. But I was deeply attached to the kids and helping raise them. As a young adolescent, the capacity of being stronger, to act, wasn't and isn't easy for anyone, even today. I knew even then that I didn't want to make trouble which could hurt the children.

I am fine now and free to talk.

This abuse happens more often with people who are in position of power. The worst abuse is that toward a child and mind games. The power of unwanted words. The power of physical unwanted advances, of unwanted bodily touches in any way shape or form.

The fact that we have a president who has been accused of similar conduct and a potential senator accused of the same, and that this Congress and Senate feel complacent and do nothing scares me. In what kind of country will my grandchildren be growing up in?

This is my story. Please tell it.

Cindy Sherman - Sherman was born in 1954 and is an artist whose photographs explore the roles of women in society and questions the viewer's values and preconceptions concerning women's identities. She consistently pushes her audiences by altering her appearance beyond recognition. Most of her works show Sherman as the model, photographer, and director. She develops and visually represents personas from fairy tales, art history, film noir, and the fashion world, challenging the genre of portraiture. Her work is included in several renowned collections throughout the world.

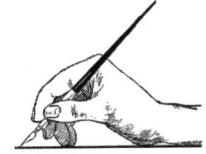

Samantha, 20, Minnesota, USA

In high school, I had this best friend. We'll call him David.

David and I were best friends for about roughly two to three years (which was a long time, considering how often I've moved around in my life). One day, we started dating. And it was AMAZING. Something important to note is that I was a virgin with a history of sexual abuse, so sex was a very iffy subject for me. And because of my past, I've always had an incredible aversion to oral sex (which I've since been working on). Just even trying sent me into a panic and we'd have to stop.

He was great about it. David never pressured me and was always kind to me. I've never been big on the soulmates thing, but he had me doubting myself. That's why I ignored all of the red flags letting me know he was cheating on me. Of course, eventually I couldn't deny it any longer and it destroyed me.

He took this as an opportunity to do a 180. He became very mentally abusive and manipulative, bringing me to a panic attack every time I was unable to have sex with him. I became desperate to sleep with him because CLEARLY that would make everything better. He would stop cheating and we'd go back to being happy, if only I could have sex with him. But because of my past, wanting to do it out of desperation, instead of lust, meant I just wasn't able to. It was like hitting a wall.

Some months passed like this and he got progressively meaner and I got progressively more broken. Eventually I hit the "fuck it" mentality. I decided I would get absolutely drunk, and that way, in the worst-case scenario, I wouldn't remember the pain, or if it didn't work, he could simply put me to bed. He was my best friend of three to four years, and boyfriend of a year at this point. I trusted him completely. He was okay with this idea, but only as long as he stayed sober "so that nothing bad happened."

So I chugged as much vodka as I could, and ended up blacking out for roughly seven hours. When I woke up, I was tied up to the point of pain. I was on my back, bound at the ankles, knees, elbows, and wrists. I was awkwardly laying on my arms and everything about the situation hurt. David was straddling my chest, with his fist in my hair, pulling it too hard, and violently facefucking me. I was still a bit drunk when I woke up, so I had absolutely no idea even who I was, let alone who he was or what was happening.

Obviously I freaked out. After some begging and crying, he finally untied me, but when questioned, he refused to tell me what all we had done. Still to this day I don't know. I spent the following few weeks in a daze. I kept finding ways to excuse it, but the more I thought back on it, the more I realized I was forcing myself to accept it.

It took me awhile to be able to leave him, but thankfully he's been out of my life for about two years now. For about a year afterwards he would come into my place of work, and threaten and degrade both me and my current boyfriend.

He even went so far as to "anonymously" call the ethics department within my company and tell them my boyfriend and I were making out on the sales floor. This could have gotten us fired, as my current boyfriend was the manager over all of the cashiers there and technically it wasn't okay that we were dating per company policy, but the managers had allowed it with the understanding that we would maintain a good work image and I would never work a register, so he would not ever be my direct boss.

I've recently moved away from that town and I am doing so much better.

I still have a hard time calling it rape. He was my best friend and I think that is the worst part.

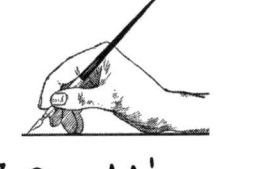

Ann, 70, Missouri, USA
#metoo

TV news recently showed a clip they thought was funny. It was a video of a very upset 9-year-old boy being forced by his mom to write a letter to Santa. He signed it "You don't know the terrible things that have happened in my life."

I was diagnosed a couple of years ago as having a form of PTSD. I have flashbacks of trying to survive being taken sexually advantage of from around the ages of 3 to 9 years old by two close family members, along with another man who married into my family. These included his older dad and teenage nephew, who was a good friend of one of my brothers.

Another was a family friend who would often stop by with hot, fresh doughnuts for the whole family. Sometimes he would pick me up and set me on his motor scooter, holding and fondling me while on the way to pick up doughnuts. I got a bad ankle burn from the scooter, from the uncovered muffler.

I also have had recent memories of a man who offered coins to me to let him look at me without clothes on. This happened more than once. Another man would let kids in his house when his wife was gone. He also gave kids coins to "look at me."

This all stopped when my family moved away from Springfield to Kansas City and I could finally fight back at 9 years old.

JM, 48, New York, USA

I was 9 years old, my parents had just announced they were separating, and as they figured it all out, I was being sexually molested by a close family friend.

My parents had me when they were 18, so no, I was not planned. They probably would never have gotten married, being very different from one another, but still their separation came as a surprise and I remember feeling very lost and confused as to what it meant for the future. I lived in NYC and my dad would go out every night to work on his new apartment, which was less than a mile away. My mom had recently met a new man, her boyfriend who would be in my life for the next 35 years (becoming my step-dad) and I was excited to spend time getting to know him.

My mom and dad had recently been contacted by a friend who they had known since their teenage years. He was a bit lost and needed a place to stay. My mom offered our couch and this man, who was also in his 20s, seemed like a big brother of sorts to me.

I was left alone at night for a few hours a few times a week and I know both my parents thought they were doing me a service, as this man enjoyed playing board games and seemed like a big kid himself. I remember the first time we were sitting together watching television, and he put his hand in an unfamiliar way on my leg.

It's a confusing feeling at such a young age, when you are longing for comfort and someone you care about makes this advance. I later came to learn he had been abused by his own father and that this is usually a learned behavior. At the time, it just felt weird, confusing, and I felt guilty for allowing him to touch me and kiss me. Most of the time we spent time together there was just a friendship of sorts (though I was 9 and he was about 23, so not a normal friendship). At times he would get closer to me and ask me questions, like if I had ever seen a man naked.

These feelings, coupled with my parents separating, definitely caused a lot of angst and mood swings in me. The man told me not to tell anyone, and he never went further than kissing or touching and asking me questions. I knew it was not okay, but at the same time I did not understand and somehow it felt okay because he cared about me, and he was close with my entire family. It was a very strange time, and once he moved out, I noticed he distanced himself very much from my family, probably feeling guilty.

I would not tell my parents about what happened until about 10 years later when I was an angry teen in high school. By that point, I could not even count how many times I was sexually approached or was the receiver of lewd comments or harassment.

Growing up in New York City, I walked often and almost everywhere. I was an attractive teenager who loved to dance and cannot remember a day I walked down the sidewalk from the ages of 14 to 25 and did NOT receive a comment from some strange man. Some of them were okay -- a man tipping his hat or saying hello. Some would give me compliments and tell me how beautiful I was and wish me a nice day.

And then there were the others. The comments ranged from comments about my breasts (at DD, they were kind of hard to keep a secret) to comments on what these strangers would like to do to me. Mind you, I was 14 years old hearing some of these comments -- I remember not even knowing what a few of the things were that were said to me. I loved living in the city, but took to wearing headphones almost everywhere to drown out the sounds and comments.

There was the one day when the comments went further. I'd had a pretty long and emotional day. I'd twisted my ankle (and was limping), and remember just feeling exhausted, weak and that things were not in a good space. I was walking down the city streets in this state, feeling ANYTHING but attractive, when I got a comment to the effect of how beautiful I was and that this guy knew what it would take to make me happy (sexually), said with a sick grin on his face. I was NOT pleased. I think I mumbled something like "I am not interested," and he started to follow me, talking non-stop about how I was a stuck-up bitch and how he could do things that would "fix" me.
I walked for a block and could not shake this guy. The faster I went, the

faster he went. I walked into a store, and he waited outside where I could not see him. It was the first time I felt real panic from a comment on the street. I eventually went into a place where there was a policeman and told him someone was bothering me, and just the cop peeking out of the store made the guy move on. I do not know what would have happened if I did not find that policeman.

I was a sophomore in college when the next occurrence happened. I was at a party at my boyfriend's house off campus, where he lived with my closest guy friends. There was a new guy on campus from Brazil, so he spoke Portuguese and did not know I had Spanish-speaking friends and knew some of the "not so nice" words in his language.

I was in the kitchen, and he and another new guy on campus looked me up and down, and I heard him clearly say what translated into English as "I want to eat her pu%$#." I remember the look of recognition on his face as he knew I understood what he had said. I felt so violated. Here I was at a place I felt comfortable, and someone could say this about me. I promptly had my closest guy friend kick him out, but he made the guy apologize to me first. It was NOT a heartfelt apology, and he even questioned why I was upset and said it was a compliment! I still had this very grossed-out feeling for days afterward. I know they were just words, but I could not wrap my head around why anyone would say that to someone else in such a crude manner. I could never look the guy in the face again.

When I went back to live in the city, the comments continued, and I got pretty good at ignoring them. I was temping for a while and had some comments thrown out here and there from other employees. While I was waiting for graduate school to start, I also tried to get some modeling jobs. That was short lived; in the month I tried to get some modeling jobs, I had one agent offer me drinks at 11 a.m. and another ask me to read and act out a pornographic script when I was there for a photo shoot possibility. It was clear this was not the path for me.

I met and dated a few people over the years. There was one guy I met, and we were to go on our first date after speaking a few times on the phone and really connecting. I remember being so excited about the date, as he was the first guy I had liked in a while. He had just separated from a longstanding relationship, and we had a lot in common. We had a wonderful time walking, going to the Central Park Zoo, and then we were going to go to my place to change and then go out to dinner. He had traveled from outside the city to visit and had brought a change of clothes.

When we got to my apartment, he kissed me and the feeling was mutual, but suddenly things were moving WAY TOO FAST. I said "STOP" clearly several times and moved his hands from where they were wandering. He would hesitate, resume kissing, but soon his hands were back where they wanted to go and being more aggressive. This did not end well. I continued to say "STOP" and tried to pull away. I had a dress on and felt like I just kept having to pull it down and he was just pulling it up in some strange tug-of-war.

It seemed like he felt it was some kind of joke or that I was not serious, even though I was serious with every fiber of my being. I remember feeling helpless, like maybe I deserved it, having this new guy to my apartment and getting date raped.

Afterward, I was crying and told him, "I said, 'no' several times, I did NOT WANT THAT." And he honestly looked surprised. He asked me if I still wanted to go to dinner and continue our date. I replied "no," that I wanted him out of there and never to see him again. He had gotten me a present on our outing and I asked him to take it with him -- telling him I wanted no memory of our date, but, of course, that memory remains. He actually looked perplexed and sad as I gave it back to him.

I do not know if the date rape guy had some sort of weird thing where he thought "no" meant "yes," but I know he left my place knowing he had done wrong.

I never even thought to press charges because I felt like women are always made to be the bad guy in this type scenario. I did have a date with him, I did let him into my apartment, I did kiss him. But no, I did not want to have sex with him and didn't even want him touching me the way he did. From all the legal shows and movies I had seen and heard about, I knew it would be me defending myself instead of telling my story and that felt more heart wrenching than I could bear.
I never understood why women are made to feel like the bad guys and

how men could not understand boundaries, but soon understood that is not all men. And sometimes it is even women who are the abusers. Men are taught how to behave with women in all sorts of relationships and they copy that behavior. Some are smart enough to question the behavior if it is abusive and make different choices as they heal their own wounds. Some repeat the patterns.

It was necessary for me to be more discerning and use more caution in dating, and this message was deeply received. I still kept my heart open, but knew that I had a lot more caution and only put myself in situations where I felt 100 percent safe.

Even with this in place, I was groped while on the massage table of a trusted healing practitioner. I learned he had also done this to many others. I warned people about him and was able to understand that just because someone has a trusted title, it does NOT make them trustworthy. It was a hard lesson, as I had considered this man a friend. Again, I know not all men were like this, but I have certainly run into a fair share in my lifetime thus far!

Since then, I have dated some wonderful men. I have a love in my life now like I never thought possible. There was a TON of healing to get through in my life to begin to trust men again. Luckily, I've always had good guys as friends, which helped restore my confidence as well.

People learn how to treat other people. From the beginning of my relationships as an adult, I set healthy boundaries and even voiced what I would and would not allow. My experiences at first made me leery of men, but secondly made me stronger in my own experience as a woman, and knowing how to set healthy boundaries and know I deserve a man who will treat me right. I would advise every woman not to settle and to know they deserve to be treated well. We all deserve to be treated well and have our boundaries respected.

I have decided to be anonymous here, as my children don't know the graphic details of all that has happened to me and I really don't need them to read them. I am very grateful this #metoo movement has empowered women to speak out about something which has been happening for far too long. It is my hope this light has been shined into the darkness -- and it will not be tolerated anymore.

I am grateful for Jyssica for putting these powerful stories together, and for each of the women and men who took the time and energy to share their own stories.

Me too -- I have been disrespected and sexually harassed as a woman, many times.

Me too -- I have a deep love for the connection women have and our strengths. My female friendships are powerful and priceless!

Me too -- let's change the world so everyone respects each other and there doesn't need to be so many secrets or fear anymore -- rather let's move into a place of love and union.

Me too -- I am so grateful to be a woman during this time when our truth is being heard to reveal a much kinder world where we WILL and DO receive the respect we deserve!

Coretta Scott King - Well known for her marriage to Martin Luther King Jr. and her work with Civil Rights, Coretta Scott King devoted much of her life to women's equality. She helped found NOW (National Organization for Women) in 1966 and played a key role in the organization's development. In her efforts for women's rights, King was notably the first woman to deliver the class day address at Harvard University.

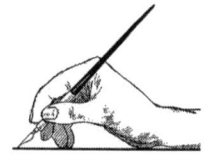

Mark, 62, New York, USA

I was 17 in the summer between high school graduation and going off to college, and I took a job as a maintenance man at a local Jewish Community Center(JCC) to earn some extra money. The position involved routine cleaning, maintenance, and painting classrooms. The head of the maintenance department took an interest in me and initially was very encouraging and kind. I thought he was a nice guy.

Over time, he began to get physically very close to me. Too close. With a smile, he would squeeze my arm or rub my shoulders, and tell me what a great job I was doing for the JCC and the community.

I am not sure I found it creepy, at least not at first, but it was certainly an uncomfortable feeling; it just didn't seem right, but I still didn't tell anyone. What if I was misinterpreting it? When I would least expect it, I would turn around and he would be right there, beaming at me and touching me.

One afternoon, after a long day of painting and other manual labor tasks, he suggested, that rather than going home all covered with paint and other chemicals, I should go to the on-site gym locker room and take a shower. And so I did. After all, it genuinely seemed like a sensible idea.

I was in the shower when he appeared.

He told me I had a beautiful body and his outstretched arm reached right for my crotch. In reaction, I grabbed him by the wrist and threatened to hit him if he didn't back off. He retreated, but I knew is was not something I could ignore.

I was not terrified because I was able to defend myself, but I certainly felt violated and shocked that someone would make a grab for me in the privacy of a shower stall.

When I got home, I told my dad, who went right down to the JCC to complain. The man was fired, but I do not think any law enforcement got involved. Certainly, no one asked me for any kind of statement.

For a considerable time after that I confused child molestation and homosexuality in my mind. I wrongly thought homosexual men were either promiscuous, predatory, or both. I pictured them engaging in sexual activities in parking lots and public restrooms, as well as preying on innocent children. When the AIDS epidemic burst forth, I was not particularly sympathetic.

During the mid- to late '90s, I began to become aware of colleagues of mine who were gay and involved in long-term committed relationships, even wearing wedding bands. I came to realize that what I thought was typical behavior was actually aberrational, and my fear and confusion had caused me to overgeneralize a group of people.

What tipped me over the edge from accepting to welcoming was when my own daughter, my first born child whom I love dearly, came out to my wife and me.

Eleanor Roosevelt - She was the premier First Lady in America to take on major responsibilities beyond hosting and entertaining in the White House. She was known to be outspoken and involved with women's issues, working with the Women's Trade Union League and the International Congress of Working Women before becoming First Lady. From 1935 to 1962, Eleanor wrote "My Day," a newspaper column which addressed women's work, equality and rights. At the time, these social issues were considered "controversial," especially for a First Lady to speak on. Eleanor Roosevelt was the first U.S. delegate to the United Nations, served as first chair of the UN Commission on Human Rights, and also chaired JFK's President's Commission on the Status of Women to promote equality and advise on women's issues.

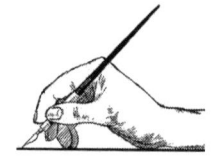

Alexis, 18, Pennsylvania, USA

Finding Your Voice

"That is how they are," I was told. As a 17-year-old girl, I was working by myself in a shop full of older men who were construction workers. It was not an enjoyable experience, especially when they were constantly making sexual remarks toward me. At my previous workplace, I was put into uncomfortable situations because of sexual harassment.

I was previously employed in a little golf shop and there was a lot of work being done to this little shop. They only had one cashier working at a time, and I was the only girl working there. There were three older men all between the ages of 40 and 50.

At first, I had no issues with them, until I started working by myself after my training ended. It started with them just saying small things such as "Wow, you look pretty today" and "Those pants look great on you." I did not think much of it besides thinking maybe they were just trying to be nice to me and make me feel welcome in the shop.

As time went on, the comments got more inappropriate. I started getting asked if I had a boyfriend and I answered yes. Then, they proceeded to ask me if my boyfriend "satisfies me." It surprised me that a 40-year-old was asking a 17-year-old about that kind of thing. I just kind of blew it off at the time, awkwardly laughed, and changed the subject. The longer I worked there, the worse the comments and questions got.

I was sitting there doing my homework one day and I got asked if I would go back to one man's house and if we could "have a good night." That alarmed me. I realized this was not a normal thing to say to a young female working by herself. I just said "no" and walked away.

The next time I worked, another man decided to slip me his phone number across the table and said, "Call me anytime, and if you need anything, and I mean anything, just call me, no strings attached." I realized then I needed to tell someone.

I first told my other coworker because my boss lived in a different state and I did not see him often. She told me "that is how they are."

I was not going to accept that. Just because they are construction workers does not mean they can talk to women however they want and it is just supposed to be okay because that is their nature. I tried to make it known what was going on, but the next time I went to work they were there again. So, clearly nothing was done.

Another girl ended up getting hired and she said they were asking her what kind of underwear she was wearing. She was too scared to speak up, so I confronted the men for her. I decided to speak up for her because I knew how she was feeling and I did not want her to feel alone and afraid, like how I was feeling because when I tried to do something about my experiences nothing got done.

Nothing changed. I was not sure what I was exactly expecting to happen, but nothing at all happened.

A third guy was alone with me in the shop one day and I was sitting there doing homework on my computer. He casually walked over to me, shut my laptop, and asked me, "What are we going to do?" I looked at him and responded with, "I am going to do my homework, please leave." He told the other two guys who walked in and were in front of me that I was throwing myself at him and I was rubbing up against him.

My boss finally came to the shop from his home and I talked to him about what was happening, and that was when something finally got done about it.

I was lucky enough for something finally to be done about my sexual harassers, but it still was not taken as seriously as it should have been because it took me speaking up three times before something finally got done.
It shows me that sexual harassment should not be taken lightly and it is a

serious matter. I hope more women and men can reach out to someone and get help if they are experiencing sexual harassment. Everyone experiencing anything along these lines needs to find their voice and not be afraid to speak out.

Elizabeth Cady Stanton - 1815-1902 - Stanton was raised in a progressive home and became involved at an early age in the abolitionist movement. She helped organize the National Women's Loyal League with Susan B. Anthony in 1863 and advocated for liberal divorce laws and reproductive self-determination. Her efforts helped bring about the 19th Amendment, giving women the right to vote in the U.S. A quote from her: "The best protection any woman can have...is courage."

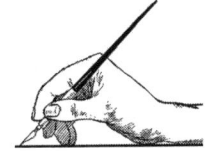

Marita M., 56, Victoria, Australia

Unprotected Sex

I grew up in a small, rural, isolated Catholic settlement in Victoria, Australia. Maryknoll was first started by a religious visionary, a Catholic priest, to get families out of the suburbs and into leading a holy and healthy rural lifestyle. My dad and mum purchased their block of land sight unseen from the plan, wanting only "the block closest to the church" for our new family home.

It's super, and I think that planning, which was put in place in the early 1950s, remains the same to this day. Prior to their marriage at Saint Augustine's Melbourne on the 31st of May 1949, Dad had been driving taxis, and was bashed and robbed, earning a head injury which led to a brain tumour which sadly later claimed his life.

The same year Mum and Dad married, Father Pooley put down his entire worldly wealth as a deposit on a square mile of virgin bushland some 70 to 80 kilometers from the GPO in Melbourne. Thus, their concept of a co-operative society was started. Everyone owned shares and the men built the houses together, then added The Holy Family Church, the presbytery for the priest to live in, a convent for the teaching nuns, and finally the school.

The school opened the year I started, 1966. Today it is the Hall. My husband and I were married in the church in 1985.

Harking back, Dad became unwell in the mid-1960s and was unable to work or drive due to "fits." So, as I was the youngest of seven (Mum and Dad used to say seven for Heaven), Dad and I hung out together all the time. He did help with the building of the school, and I used to take over his morning tea and lunch, and hang out with the men as they built "my school." I can recall these days very clearly today, even though I was only 4 years old.

As I turned 5 mid-year, it was decided that I was forward enough with socializing and reading to start school earlier rather than later. Mum had been a teacher herself in her early 20s, teaching form 6 or "leaving" or VCE, as we call it here now. She was teaching at a country (Colac) high school, the final year of secondary for students who were nearly her own age, until she was called back to Melbourne by a priest, who was a close friend and her "scholastic advisor." He decreed she was a "wasted talent" and asked her to come back to the city.

Being the youngest of seven, she thought I was well and truly ready to start school, so I did. Dad took me over on my first day and I knew all the other working men's daughters from Mass on Sundays, Tuesdays, and Thursdays. So, I wasn't afraid, but I would rather have spent my time with Dad. At the end of my sixth year on this Earth he would be dead and buried, leaving Mum alone as a widow with seven children under 17 years of age. Her elderly mother, my only living grandparent who I ever got to meet, lived nearby, and as Mum was an only child, Mum had sole responsibility for her, too.

Toward the end of 1968, with Dad gone, my mum was away sick, and I was at home with my brothers and Gran. She would have been 84 at the time and I was 7 years old. I was supposed to be picked up and have a holiday in Melbourne with my godmother, who lived in Rosanna and I had been to her place before. It turns out they came from Elsternwick previously, where Maryknoll's founder had also been the former parish priest.

There was a change of plans, and I was standing out in the front with Gran when this big dark car arrived with a woman and three young boys. I was used to boys, as I had five older brothers. But, I recall to this day how I felt VERY apprehensive and shrank back, and I now always tell my own four children to NEVER ignore your gut instinct, as it will never let you down.

Having no say, I left in the car with this woman I didn't know, her two sons, who were 11 and 14, and the other boy, who was an aborigine juvenile delinquent, a dark youth of 14 who was TROUBLE. I found out later that he was the only absconder from two remand centers in 1968, and I was about to be at his mercy. We had no television at home and I was a very sheltered and naive child, wanted and loved by my family. My life was about to be turned on its head.

When we returned to Elsternwick, the woman dressed me in trousers. This was very against my mother's teachings and wishes, and I knew Mum would be very unhappy, but sadly for both of us, she wasn't here. From the day I was born until the day they both died (Mum and Gran), I never saw either of them dressed in pants, and Gran wasn't even a Catholic.

This woman put me to bed that night; she very excitingly, had a radio, and instructed me to turn it off before I fell asleep and then she left the room in darkness.

Then there was a hand over my mouth! It was the aborigine, eugene (I refuse to use a capital, as I have no respect for him). The sexual abuse of a small scared child, away from her mum and family for the first time, was about to start. I was terrified to say the least.

In the morning, the mother came in and was cross to me because the radio was still on. I did not know these people. She dressed me in pants and sent me with the boys. Every day I was there, things escalated in a sexual nature from that point on.

Due to the fact that I am STILL being threatened, I shall name her older son as con (a name I think suits him perfectly). Now here is a person who was in his second year at a top private Catholic secondary college near Melbourne, while I was in grade two. He was in a position to shield and protect me from the evil or go along with it. He chose to go along with it, and therefore he has always been the person I have held a deep and great hatred for.

He was at me himself, raping me in their backyard, asking me about babies and where they came from, and did I want one? I was just a child! Threatening me not to tell, or "I would get into trouble."

Having finally seen a counsellor in 2012, after reporting the abuse to the police, the counsellor shook her head and sadly said, "You would have been exhausted as a child at night; you would've been hyper vigilant. What happened next?"

Anyway, back to the house of horrors. The mother never said, "Oh, you come and make cookies in the kitchen with me." No, she sent me off with the "boys" and I might add with me being their "honeymoon child" they were really happy to take me. So, after a week or 10 days of night time visits and other funny stuff, I was loaded onto the back of a bike and we headed off to the beach.

I loved water, but swimming wasn't on their minds. The boys were looking for a secluded place to take me where they would be unseen. At first, they looked at a big unlit bonfire, wondering if I could be taken in there. As they were discussing this, a man appeared, carrying a can and walking toward the fire. He doused it with fuel and set it alight! Wow, so scary -- five minutes earlier we would have all been in there, them trying desperately to be unseen, as of course they knew what they were doing was wrong.

So, then they took me under a bridge and I felt just like Alice falling down the rabbit hole, as things were getting weirder and weirder. The younger brother was posted as a lookout, and eugene and con removed my clothes and exposed themselves and both raped me.

I had never seen a penis! All was such a shock to my senses, it was really overwhelming! I knew "rude" was wrong. We all grew up in a very proper household with no alcohol or swearing, no nudity, only lots of praying on bended knees, going to Mass, saying rosaries, and Our Lady was Mum's favorite. The color blue, purity, chastity, virgins, immaculate conceptions, etc. This was what I'd come from and what I would go back into. Just so sad for me and my mother.

Despite being threatened, I think I spoke up at the kitchen table where the mother and father, and the three youths and I ate dinner in the kitchen together each night. I was promptly removed from the home and taken by a most wonderful lady called Mrs. Copley, who lived in a nearby suburb (Kew) and had my older brother Bill living with her. I was so pleased to see him, as we had always been close as siblings.

Her kindness at the time remains with me to this day. She would get down to my level to speak to me and hug me. She took me shopping in Melbourne, where we got separated and I just stood in a doorway watching all the big people dashing around me. She found me and was distraught. She took me shopping at Myers and it was so kind of her. As a small country kid, this was super, but I did something I had never done before. I KNEW stealing was wrong, but I stole a small green china frog. She later found this in my shiny black shoe (first communion footwear) and knelt down in front of me with the frog in her hand. I just felt so awful, I can remember this so clearly to this day.

My brothers tell me about Mrs. Copley today. She's a legend! My older brother Bill said she had to stay with us often after Dad died and she enrolled him in a top private primary school and got him a uniform. My older brother Gerard recalls her visiting Mum at Maryknoll and Mum was complaining about "the boys" driving their old bombs on the road, as Gerard came into the kitchen. He said she had a Chevy or a Cadillac herself and she promptly threw him the keys and said, "Take my car for a spin." Gotta love THAT woman!

When she took me from the house of horrors, all those adults knew what had happened to me. The family I'd been staying with had a white rabbit and I had taken comfort with that animal, so the boys said, "Oh, you can have the rabbit, we don't want it." So I had this white rabbit when I left them ... just like the adventures of Alice in Wonderland, but only much much worse, as I realise now those boys stole my innocence and effectively ended my childhood with their crude and selfish actions.

Of course, when I finally returned home to Mum with Bill, my life was to never be the same. I knew, even at that tender age, that what had happened to me was NOT a badge of honor nor something to be proud of. So, with Mum saying we were never to speak of the events, I didn't, thus creating a golden shield of ongoing silence for my perpetrators! This, sadly, had me deceiving all my close neighbors and childhood friends, and keeping such a secret down inside for someone so young does horrible damage.

I had done nothing wrong! It took until I finally went to the police and reported it in 2012 (without telling anyone) for me to suddenly realise this. When it all started to slowly come out, my life growing up made much more sense, as some of my behavior was bizarre, to say the least. I was VERY angry when I came to the realization of what those unsupervised youths had done to me!

Strangely, the police eventually found all three alive and well today, and the sort of boys they were then reflects the sort of men they became. They tried taking the high moral ground and denied everything! This has worked, to a point, as I have been able to welcome them all back into my nightmare.

The aborigine lives on the taxpayer and has led a life of crime. I've even found him in print, stating that it started at 14 years of age; yes, I know what he was doing. While I hated him and (his name means "well born" in Greek) with a passion growing up, I never really focused on him that much, but more so on the older brother, "con." His younger brother, "the lookout," also has a criminal record and lives in another state of Australia. The police in the investigation flew to the other side of the country and interviewed him. He acknowledged eugene, while denying my existence.

If I was a little country lass living way up in the bush, how was I able to tell the SOCIT team this person existed? I have that family's home in my sister's address book and I knew they later moved. So, when I went to the police and finally reported it after Mum died, how could or would I have this knowledge? Via a typo my brother made on Mum's obituary in December 2008.

Let's say I told them "johnlan," but it was really "johnellan." Because that is what I took to the police to make my report. They had trouble finding whether the boys existed and I was hassling them by saying things like, "Oh, and you call yourselves detectives?" My sister helped with the spelling and their address once the police made it clear they needed more than just the information I had.

After I spoke up, it gradually gained momentum, and I was really overwhelmed with the amount of love and support I have received from friends and family, and even perfect strangers. I was asked by my Melbourne law firm to get character references for the civil case, and I actually sent them over 100 of them for my husband and me, until they asked me to stop.

Sadly, I have never received any court case trial, either criminal or civil. When it looked like the police investigation might stall and I had found "con" online, I announced to the lawmen, "I'm going to confront him myself." They said I couldn't do that, but I replied, "He has a public place, who is going to stop me?"

Luckily, he wasn't there the day I went, and I left a note for him. He responded via his lawyer and they called a meeting with me. Best hour of my life! I had waited so long for that day! At the end of the hour, he bolted from the room after admitting nothing and his lawyer threatened me before he, too, left the room. I thought it was so funny.

I can now reflect upon my childhood. After "he" refused to acknowledge me or what he did to me when he was twice my age, I called for my school reports. My second secondary school report arrived, and it is a really distressing read of a young adolescent child crying out for help and failing in a most spectacular fashion. Then I left all formal schooling at the age of 12, part way through year 8 or form 2.

Given that my mother was university educated and a prolific author of note herself, one asks oneself what the hell happened? Clearly this mother believes in education for girls. I consulted my five older brothers one afternoon, all in a row, so they spoke directly to me before speaking to each other, as I knew they would later. It seems as though Mum's burden of carrying what had happened to me was too much and she "confessed" to two of them, therefore, they knew and submitted statutory declarations.

This sadly was still not enough evidence to get me into court, where I was seeking a voice for my smaller self. In fact, to not be heard, three male judges (I call them the three wise men) overruled a female County Court judge, who had previously ruled that my case would go to trial in October 2017. They then saddled me with the court costs of well over $100,000 for trying.

So, five years after going to the police, I sat down and wrote out a personal check to my police-identified rapist, which he did cash.

This is what justice for women in Australia looks like today. I am embarrassed to be one. Is this how society treats us when we speak up?

In closing, I say that I do have documents stating that none of our four children ever attended any school camps or sleepovers. They attended our local primary school for a total of 23 years, and two still attend the local high school. All are or have been really good students who love school.

When my sad story finally came out, a Murphy child went on a school camp to Germany! That took some explaining! That has been one joy of shedding these long held dirty secrets.

All I can say is that as a mother, it must have been a subconscious protection mechanism, trying to shield my own children from the horrors I had been forced to experience.

Emmeline Pankhurst - *Pankhurst founded the Women's Social and Political Union in the United Kingdom, known as the Suffragettes. She was imprisoned several times and fought to enfranchise women with the right to vote. The British Parliament granted women limited suffrage in 1918, and only after Pankhurst died in 1928 were they given full voting rights. She said, "We have to free half of the human race, the women, so that they can help to free the other half."*

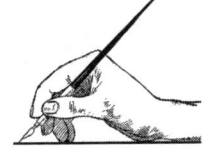

Leta, 34, California, USA

Over 10 years ago now, I started a creative writing project. When I joined LinkedIn, I found there were creative writing groups and thought they could really help me get better and learn. I could get professional help in shaping the social customs of my world, which I wanted to be a universal matriarchy with various cultures. All I learned is there are people who do not deserve to be professionals.

When I asked how a society would be different with women who give birth but take on leadership roles while men take on nurturing ones, I got not one, but three posts that women could never be leaders or even workers due to constant pregnancy.

I was told no woman has accomplished anything like that in history. When I responded with actual evidence of working women and historical female leaders and scientists, both I and they were insulted, with one man saying those women caused more problems than help by doing those things. When I ignored him, he kept replying, as I could not block him.

I did what any sane person on social media would do. I reported them. When nothing happened, I reported the posts again. When a week went by, I messaged the moderators. They all said they saw nothing wrong and one asked me to apologize to him.

About five years ago, I was on Reddit. Someone stalked me for a week to protest nearly any post I made because I made a comment that he could make up what he wanted to, but the strength difference between men and women bodybuilders was only in the top 5 percent of both sexes. He protested, saying no woman could outrun him or out bench-press him. Not a certain woman or even just "an athlete," but any woman.

This year, I joined a writing group called Marvel's Non-Canon Universe. It was small and just about characters in the Marvel universe. I pushed myself to edit everything for others so we could post stories soon. I was eager to help with ideas. The moderators cheered everyone on saying, "We just want everyone to have fun."

Then the moderators brought in a friend of theirs. The project was for everyone to work together. All the stories were to be in the same place and incorporate (or at least mention) events from each others' stories. It was meant to be collaboration. The friend didn't want to. At all. He didn't want to compromise, listen, or even do basic research into characters. He refused to work with my story, which I had several chapters of which I had already written.

I was a moderator, but it would look wrong to tell him to stop, as it would look like an abuse of power. So, again, I turned to the other moderators. They suddenly changed to "He's [writing] the A-lister" and "Well, you should have thought about this when you chose an unpopular character. Why didn't you choose an A-list character?"

Why not? Because I wanted to write a character who would interact with several strong women, that's why. Why didn't I write about those women? Because the moderators and their friend shut down any use of most of them and the one single female character left was also not an A-list character.

I quit the group and they got angry I didn't bow to their whims. They acted like dictators and got mad I called them such. One moderator was angry that I said they mistreated me and insulted me for saying so. He even made a proxy account and had a troll stalk me to insult me on a Reddit forum about being bullied -- yes, he bullied me on a bullying forum and said he was right to do so.

Then I remembered there was only one other female in the group. She never wrote A-listers. I looked up A-list characters. The only female character was written by the bullying moderator, and he only wrote her as a cheerleader for a male character. The friend wrote two other females as just victims.

He was careful not to get caught saying it, but he and his group hated women.

Anonymous, 14, Minnesota, USA

I'm 14 years old. The majority of my sexual abuse happened two years ago, when I was 12 years old, at school.

My abuser still goes to my school with me and I still have to see him everyday. I feel myself tense up and all of the hairs on my back stand up. He used to make comments to me, shout at me, and try to grab my breasts and my vagina. He still tries to do some of those things. He will come up to me, grab my hand, talk to me.

I'm not saying what he did was right, but that's not the thing which bothers me the most. It's the fact that he is twice my size and could easily rape or hurt me.

I go to school in fear of what he could do to me. He took away my innocence. I no longer feel safe.

It's not as bad now as it used to be. He never did anything worse. One of the administrators at school knows, and my parents knew about the original abuse, but not as much about what is going on now. I have an amazing support system and I talk with two rape crisis counselors, too.

Very few people know about it, though. Almost no one knows about all of the repercussions of my abuse. I am depressed and I have anxiety. Some days it just feels as though I'm drowning; like I'm gasping for air. But it won't always be this way.

I know it will get better. It made me stronger.

#MeToo

Melissa D., 65, New York, USA

INCIDENT #1 –Occurred in Orange County, California

I was in my mid-20s and single, enjoying life one day at a time. I lived alone, worked full time, and enjoyed going out at night. I was a very naïve and trusting person. I was not street-wise, not even close. My parents never taught me the facts of life or, for that matter, anything about life. I was learning as I went along in my daily life.

Because of my sheltered life growing up, I hadn't dated very much. I had been involved with one man for about six months and we had recently gone our separate ways. It was no big deal; we both realized we were too young to be so involved and decided it was time to move on.

Back in those days, I would go to a restaurant which had a cocktail lounge with live entertainment (usually a solo acoustic guitarist). I had a couple of friends who lived nearby, so we would usually meet on the weekends to enjoy a few drinks and the live entertainment.

There was one man in particular who seemed to be a regular, like my friends and me. He dressed very well, carried himself as if he were extremely confident, and he was good looking. We found ourselves looking at each other periodically over the next few months when were both at the lounge.

I don't recall how it happened, but one night we ended up talking. We may have spoken before that night, but I don't remember. This night, however, I do recall speaking with him, or should I say listening to him – as he spoke about himself and his career. He spoke of awards, pictures and other "impressive" things in his life. Although I was not impressed with his accomplishments, I did enjoy hearing his stories.

Again, I don't remember exactly what happened, but I do remember ending up at his apartment to see his awards and pictures. While there, I clearly remember him asking me if I wanted anything to drink. Since we had already been at the cocktail lounge, I said I wanted water as I'd already had a few drinks. He went to his kitchen as I sat on his living room couch perusing his photo album. He returned with a glass of water for me. That was the last thing I remember before waking up in his bedroom.

As I laid on my back on his bed, I remember him saying something to me and all I could do was think to myself that I could not do what he was telling me to do. I don't remember if I was able to speak out loud. I do remember knowing I could not think clearly. He was on top of me and I was falling off the bed, head first. He jumped off the bed to try to catch me. I hit the floor and an exercise machine that was next to his bed.

That is all I remember of that night. I have no recollection of when or how I got home.

It was about three months later before I saw him again at the cocktail lounge. I had no memory of that night and, for some unknown reason at that time, had no interest in speaking with him. Looking back, I can only guess that I figured I was moving on with my life and he was not to be a part of it.

It wasn't until about a year later during a casual conversation with a girlfriend, that I realized he had drugged and raped me. My girlfriend said something during our chat, and out of nowhere, the memories of that night came flooding back to me. Those memories had been hidden for a year – and something she said during our casual conversation must have caused that evening to come back to me.

There was absolutely no need for him to drug and rape me. I was obviously interested in him. Would I have had sex with him? My guess is probably yes. Again, I was very naïve and thought he was very handsome. He appeared to be the perfect gentleman. Why wouldn't I want to be with someone like that?

I may have been naïve, but I wasn't stupid. I still remember his face, his full name and his birthday month (he did brag about how his initials matched the first three letters of his birth month). I will never forget.

I cannot undo what happened. At this point in my life, I can only hope that I was his last victim. If I wasn't, I hope someone more streetwise than I was able to put him where he belongs – in prison, with a record as a registered sex offender.

My advice today to anyone who is in a similar situation is to speak up as soon as you realize what happened. Do not wait. There is a statute of limitations on whatever the crime was. Stop him from doing his harm to someone else before time runs out. If he did it once, he just may do it again. If you do not report it, you may not be the last victim. SPEAK UP! SAY SOMETHING!

INCIDENT #2 – Occurred in Alabama, USA
NO – you may NOT hug me!

Oh, how I wish I had said that. I was in my early 30s and it had been two years since I had moved to a new state. My spouse of five years was offered a grant to pursue his Ph.D. I had left the workforce for a while to raise our two children and help my spouse settle into his new academic routine, and was ready to go back to work. I applied for and was offered a position at his university.

It was my first day on the job. My boss was taking me around the floor of our department introducing me to some of the more prominent staff members. One of them was an older man. As I look back on that day, I would guess he was in his late 50s, maybe early 60s. As my boss was introducing me to him, he stepped forward and hugged me.

I was totally taken by surprise. I had never experienced anything like that before and I froze. As he stepped away, my boss pulled me away and said he does that with all new staff members.

I didn't know what to say or do. I was completely dumbfounded. Now, if that were to happen to me again, I know exactly what I would do and say. Although my desired reaction would be a knee-jerk one, yes, pun intended, I would not do so, unless I had no other choice. My first choice would be to, without any hesitation, push him away, and hard. At the same time, I would quite firmly say "NO – you may NOT hug me." If I could not push him away, I would resort to the knee-jerk reaction. And then walk away.

In either case, I would make it clear that his actions were not welcomed and extremely inappropriate. I would end the encounter with a word of advice to him – do it again and I will press charges. Period. That simple. Oh, how I wish I had done that back then.

My word of advice – it is never too late to learn how to conduct yourself in various situations. Do not ever let someone do something to you that you do not want done. SPEAK UP! SAY SOMETHING!

Frederick Douglass – 1888 speech, "I believe no man, however gifted with thought and speech, can voice the wrongs and present the demands of women with the skill and effect, with the power and authority of woman herself. The man struck is the man to cry out. Woman ... is her own best representative."

Sharine, 54, California, USA

I have two stories.

#1

When I was 15 years old, I was raped by my older brother's best friend. Our parents were out of town on a Saturday night in October, and my brother, then 18 and a senior in high school, decided to have a house party. It was relatively small, perhaps a dozen people who were mostly his friends. I invited one of my female friends, Tiffany.

I was not a drinker and rarely partied, even though I ran with the so-called "popular" kids, mostly athletes and cheerleaders. But at this party, I felt safe because I was at home, so I sipped on cheap beer, watching carefully how much I consumed. After about an hour, some of the girls said they were going to a bar in the neighboring town, and invited my friend and me to join them. (This was in rural Wisconsin in the 1970s, when it was easy to get into a bar if you were under the drinking age, which was 18, and especially if you were female. I never saw a girl get asked for her ID.)

At the bar, I bought a glass of cheap wine; everyone else was doing shots with beer chasers. Tiffany had a mixed drink and was flirting with men sitting at the bar. We stayed for an hour, maybe, then went back to my house. There, my brother, his best friend, Gene, and a couple other guys were all drinking hard liquor. I thought I heard someone talk about doing "blow," but didn't actually seeing any cocaine. People were getting very drunk, and a bunch of them, including Tiffany, piled into cars to go to another party.

My brother stayed back, along with his friend Gene, who was from a neighboring town, and they were really quite wasted, which made me uncomfortable. I went upstairs to my bedroom, then I decided to use the bathroom, which was downstairs near the kitchen where my brother and Gene sat at the table, still drinking. When I came out of the bathroom, I noticed that Gene wasn't in the kitchen. I thought he had left or stepped outside to pee, since there was only one bathroom in our house. My brother was now passed out at the table, and I tried to wake him, but he only mumbled and let his head fall back on the table.

As I walked back through the dark living room to go to the stairs, Gene reached out of the darkness and pulled me onto the sofa. At first, he was kissing me, and I was okay with that. I had been physically attracted to him but hadn't acted on my feelings because he was dating one of the "tough" girls from my school who was a year older than I was. I knew better than to cross one of these girls. As Gene and I were kissing, we rolled onto the floor, it was kind of funny and I laughed, but he did not. He started unbuttoning my shirt; he kissed my breasts. I was still fine, if a bit uncomfortable.

Suddenly, as though in one quick motion, he unzipped my jeans and pulled them off along with my panties. He got on top of me and pried open my legs, shoving his hard penis at my vagina. I used the muscles of my inner thighs and buttocks to keep my vagina closed. I said, "No, no" over and over, and tried pushing him off me. Then he grabbed my wrists and forced my hands over my head, pinning them to the floor. He said, very aggressively, "Let me in." I shook my head back and forth, and said "no" again. Then I stared directly into his eyes and he used his other hand to violently shove my head to one side, all the while still trying to force his penis into my vagina. I used all of my mental and physical energy to keep my vagina closed, and I said out loud, "No, not like this." I had not had intercourse yet, and I wanted my first time to be special.

After some unquantifiable time, he passed out on top of me. I remember that the weight of his body on mine felt unfathomable, crushing. I remember feeling panicked that I could barely breathe and could not move beneath him.

Eventually, when I realized that he was not going to wake up, I was able to move enough so his body rolled off onto the floor. But I was still motionless, afraid that he would awaken and try again, or perhaps beat me. I don't know if I laid there for two minutes or two hours.

When I rose, I went to the bathroom, numb and unable to urinate at first because the muscles in my lower body were spasming from my efforts to keep his penis from penetrating my vagina. Finally, the urine came out. I washed my hands, face, and entire bottom, carefully exited the bathroom to see my brother still passed out, and slipped past Gene's sleeping body. I locked my bedroom door, feeling as though my brother had betrayed me. I don't remember if I slept or not, but I do recall feeling afraid that Gene would try to break into my room and hurt me.

In the morning, I called Tiffany and confided in her. Later in the day, my sister came home from her sleepover the night before, and I told her what had happened. I never mentioned it to my brother or to my parents when they came home. I never considered reporting it to any authorities. I felt like somehow I had caused Gene to assault me. I had the typical thoughts: I was dressed too provocatively; I was being flirty; I was drinking alcohol. I felt dirty, ashamed, and that I was to blame.

But it got worse.

The following morning, I was at my school locker before first period when I heard a female voice behind me say, "Hey, [my last name], you fucking slut. You seduced my boyfriend."

The blood ran from my body. I turned to see Gene's girlfriend, Bethany, with six of her tough-girl friends. They looked seriously angry, a mighty phalanx of big, bad chicks with a score to settle. As I began to form a rebuttal, I saw Tiffany, whose locker was maybe eight feet away, quickly turn and rush down the hall away from the scene, making it obvious that she had told Bethany my story.

A crowd was gathering, and I felt my face turn red. Bethany continued to yell at me, "You goddamn whore! You f*cking seduced Gene. I'm gonna f*cking kill you."

I tried to defend myself. "I did not seduce him; he came on to me," I said, as if the truth was going to change her mind.

"Who do you think you are, you stupid slut?" she screamed, "God, I swear I'm going to f*ck you up."
Out of the corner of my right eye, I could see the English teacher, Mrs. A,

just standing in the library doorway a few feet away, watching the scene and doing absolutely nothing. Her daughter was one of my closest friends. Bethany kept screaming: "You f*cking bitch. Whore. Slut."

Some of the "popular" guys in my class began whooping. They could have stopped the ordeal by just walking over to these girls and saying, "beat it, chicks," but they egged the girls on. None of my female friends stood up to protect me. The betrayal was stacking up like thousand-pound boulders, crushing my former illusion of safety and security. My whole world was crashing down on me. And it would never be the same.

The following May, my brother graduated from high school and my family had the requisite graduation party for him at our home. It was more of an open house, with people coming and going, enjoying the beautiful late May afternoon in our green-grass yard. I greeted a few family friends, but I felt bored so I went into our new family room, which my dad and a local contractor had built and finished in time for the party. I sat alone on the new couch in the bright sun, looking out through the patio doors at the vast fields of our ranch.

Suddenly, Gene walked in and sat in the chair directly across from me. He did not greet me, just sat there looking at me, completely wordless and without expression. It didn't register with me. Seven months after he sexually assaulted me, I no longer remembered that it had happened; I had repressed the memory. But I distinctly remember thinking, "I don't know why, but I want him dead." This disturbed me even more. Then, after a few minutes of him staring at me in silence, he simply got up and walked back out to the party in the front yard. That was the first time I saw him after the assault, and I never saw him again.

About two weeks after the grad party, Gene died alone in a fire in his house — and for the next 10 years I was in repression; I actually felt like I had killed him. I kept waiting for the police to show up at our door and arrest me for murdering him. I wonder now what kind of bizarre guilt trip was going on in my psyche, and how much of my energy was spent in protecting me from remembering.

On a first date at an Italian restaurant, 10 years later when I was living in

Los Angeles near UCLA, my date expressed concern that I had no car and got around on foot.

"You could get raped," he said gravely.

Suddenly, I slammed my fist on our dining table and yelled, "Don't tell me about rape. I've been raped and I know what it's like." We stared at each other in silence. After a moment, I said, "I have?" The floodgates were opened.

Less than a year later, I took a series of personal and professional development seminars that were helpful in being gentle on myself as I explored the repressed memories and emotional upheaval. I also met many wonderful facilitators and participants, and we helped each other work through our stuff, several of whom became close friends.

Twenty-ish years later, my sister, who still lives in our hometown, said she and Bethany got into a long conversation one day, and Bethany told her how sorry she was that she was abusive to me in front of my classmates and teachers. I'm glad she apologized, but it would have been better if she had simply asked me what happened in a private conversation instead of screaming insults and accusations at me in front of my classmates and teachers.

Our culture is so messed up that women are frequently the ones furthering the abuse by letting men off the hook. It compounds the tragedy.

#2

Fast forward to me at 51 years old, married with a fulfilling work and social life, healthy and happy. My husband and I met with friends in Los Angeles, and another friend, Carl, happened to be traveling through L.A. that evening, so he joined us as well. We met at a restaurant for dinner and live music. I had told Carl I wanted to help pay for our other friends' meals as a gift, so he and I stayed in the dining room to work out the tab while everyone else went to the lounge. I got up to use the ladies room.

Back at the table, as we tallied up, Carl suddenly nudged up to me and said, "I've always thought that you are a nice looking lady, but tonight, seeing you all dressed up, well, you're hot." I joked it off, saying, "I clean up real good." A minute later, he moved even closer to me, "Damn, you are beautiful." I said, "Wow, thanks for the compliment." He continued, "You're kind of turning me on."

At that moment, I was extremely uncomfortable. I turned to look at my husband, who was sitting about 25 feet away, drinking way too much. I laughed off Carl's comment, just as the server came to finish up the bill, and we carried our wine glasses to the lounge. I slipped into the booth next to my husband, and Carl found a spot next to our friend Mary. Carl was there without his wife, who had elected not to travel with him on this particular trip.

The live music started and a few of us danced. We stayed for about an hour. As we were all getting ready to go our separate ways, Carl suggested that my husband and me, and the couple we were staying with all go to his hotel suite nearby to rest and stop drinking before making the 45-minute drive. We all agreed this would be a good thing, so that's what we did. My husband was pretty drunk, so I drove his car with the five of us in it to the hotel about five minutes away.

When we got to the hotel room, our female friend and I seemed really loose in a way that I don't recall feeling before. Later, I suspected Carl drugged us in our wine back at the restaurant. Carl broke out a case of wine. I thought, "This is crazy, we came here to sober up." I let him pour a glass for me, but I only drank a few sips. I suddenly got very tired, which is very strange behavior for me. I decided to rest in one of the two double beds in the adjoining bedroom area. My husband was drunk, so I showed him where I would be sleeping in case he wanted to lay down with me.

I woke up to what I thought was my husband groping my naked body (I do not remember undressing completely) and trying to insert his finger in my vagina. I reached back to stop him, and realized that it was Carl. I froze, but eventually slid out of the bed, wrapped in a sheet. I saw my clothing, jewelry, and purse on the floor next to the bed, so I grabbed it all and went to the bathroom. I sat on the toilet and felt like I was going to vomit, and when I wiped my bottom, I felt a wave of sickness roll through my body. I dressed and went to wake my husband and our two friends in the sitting area. We stood at the end of Carl's bed, and I said, loudly and abrasively, "Carl. We are leaving." He sat up halfway, mumbled something incoherent, and we walked out. On the way home, I shared what happened.

The next morning, the four of us met up with Mary and her husband for a pool party, and we all talked about the prior evening. Mary said Carl had fondled her arm, shoulder, back, and neck while seated next to her in the lounge. Mary's husband said Carl told him that he regularly has sexual relations with many women on his business travels, "A different woman in every city." We were all in shock at how the night went and what we learned about Carl. My husband and I had been friends with him and his family for 10 years. Carl always had a distinct swagger, and he frequently talked down to his wife, who a few months before had gotten huge breast implants at the age of 53.

When my husband and I returned home, he called and confronted Carl, who claimed he must have been really drunk and he never meant for that to happen. He said he didn't want to lose our friendship. But he never said he was sorry, and he never asked to see me to apologize. If he had, I told my husband I probably would have given him a second chance, but he didn't. I am aware that not expressing remorse is the sign of a sociopath, and I wasn't going to dig myself in deeper with that kind of person. Also, I told my husband Carl had betrayed him as much as me, because he knew my husband was near blackout drunk that night.

Some people I told said I should tell Carl's wife and then report him to the police. I said to each of them, "I'm not stupid. I know the statistics. And I will not drag myself and my husband through the nightmare of being blamed and shamed, only to have Carl walk free." Also, I am not interested in finding out whether Carl and his family are vindictive and willing to retaliate somehow. I know those are the reasons why sexual assault survivors don't report, and it further sickens me, but I could not bring myself to further burden my life with the likely results.

I honestly think, reflecting back on all the years of knowing Carl, he was grooming me for just such an opportunity, and that I'm not the only one.

Michelle, Age 36, Texas, USA

The #MeToo movement has been horrifying to witness. I've read story after story about people who have experienced sexual assault and degradation at the hands of the opposite sex. For me, it has brought back my own experience with assault quite vividly. I've kept the horrible memory of that night safely tucked away for many years, even from the ones who love me most. I've done so for fear of them looking at me differently for discussing something that is perceived as taboo and even impolite to talk about.

I haven't wanted to think about it. It took me years to accept what had happened to me, and I spent so long just feeling angry, embarrassed, and ashamed. Angry that I didn't think it was rape because it didn't leave any visible marks of violence on my body. Angry over the constant nightmares of that hot breath on my face. Angry that I did nothing at the time, which meant another poor woman would likely be subjected to the same trauma. Angry that I allowed myself to believe it was all my fault for far too long. Embarrassed because I'd had too much to drink. Ashamed I was stupid enough to be alone with this person who I didn't know well enough to trust.

Angry. Embarrassed. Ashamed.

No more.

Sharing this really isn't an act of bravery. It's an act of necessity. The topic of sexual assault should not be one that makes us squirm and quick to hush. It's very real and happens far too often. Anyone you know, man or woman, may have suffered an experience like mine. What you choose to do about it is up to you, but I would ask that you do something. Whether it's calling out the jerk who catcalled a woman in front of you, standing up for someone too scared to stand up for themselves, or just listening to someone who needs support; do something.

I will share my story with my son and I won't shy away from the topic just because it's uncomfortable. I will proactively keep him empowered by talking to him and keeping him informed. I won't tolerate someone sexually degrading a woman or man if I happen to bear witness to this type of behavior. This experience doesn't define any part of me or make me a less phenomenal woman.

Thanks for taking the time to read this. Be kind to each other. God bless.

Frida Kahlo - *Kahlo painted brutally honest self-portraits. Throughout her life she tolerated extreme, physical pain and had more than 35 operations all told. She was also a rebel, a feminist, and a revolutionary. Although she is the subject of many of her paintings, the topics address infertility, gender equality, miscarriages, heartbreak, and sickness. She displayed her bisexuality publically, and had an open marriage with her husband, painter Diego Rivera. She defied gender stereotypes, glorifying her 'masculine' qualities in her paintings and not proscribing to cultural or gender norms. She also explored and communicated significantly intimate female experiences such as miscarriages, pregnancy, menstruation, breastfeeding, infertility, and sexual orgasms. She was very politically active, being an atheist and a proud communist.*

Michael L., 72 years old, Kansas, USA
Searching For Approval

This is a story of pain and suffering. My sister was born out of wedlock a year and a half before my parents were married and three years before I was born.

Our dad was the baby of three, with two older sisters who doted on him after two brothers died shortly after their births. Our mother was the youngest of four girls whose mother got them together and told them she didn't want them, and the only reason she had them was because their father wanted children. Mom was a country bumpkin who, although Mormon, got pregnant at 16. Dad left for the Army shortly after the pregnancy and became a paratrooper.

Ten years later we were all in Germany where he was stationed. My sister walked in on Dad and my mother's best friend having sex. She was sworn to secrecy. Nine months later, a child was born, whom we all thought was the friend's and her husband. I found out the truth nine years later while I was telling my mother I was going to marry my girlfriend and she thought that was the best time to tell me I had a half-brother in Texas.

When we were at Fort Bragg and my sister was 12, my dad started forcing her to perform oral sex on him while he molested her. That went on once in a while for years. She tried to tell my mother what was happening, and Mom said she told our dad to stop. He did not.

Then we moved to the Marine base at Quantico, Virginia, where Dad was being transferred. My mom, me, and my three younger brothers moved to a new house while my sister stayed with a friend as she finished up her sophomore year in high school. My dad moved into the BOQ (Bachelor Officers' Quarters) while he finished up his work at Fort Bragg in preparation of the transfer.

On a Friday night, his outfit was having a going-away party where they were to award him the Army Commendation medal. Because my mom was in Virginia with us, he decided to take my 16-year-old sister with him that night. He drank a lot, as usual, and with the lateness of the party, talked a guy into letting him borrow his MG sports car to take my sister home and get something to eat.

It was raining as they headed to the late-night hamburger joint and Dad proposed a change -- that they both go back to the BOQ so he could have sex with her. She remembers saying "no-no-no" in her head and thinking she wished he were dead. She finally screwed up enough courage to say "NO!"

In response, he stomped on the gas and they went careening through a stop sign and across a four-lane divided intersection. A bystander said sparks flew out from the undercarriage hitting the ground, and then they drove across a small patch of land and disappeared over a cliff.

When the car hit, it threw my sister out and onto the railroad tracks, breaking her legs. Then the car flipped into the air and landed over her, just missing squashing her comatose body. The steering wheel went through my dad, but the wet sand saved my sister. Her head was in water, but the guy who saw them go over scrambled down the cliff and pulled her head out, saving her life. He then went for help.

The next day, we got a telegram saying our dad was dead and my sister was on life support in the hospital. My mom, me, and my next younger brother flew down to Fort Bragg that day. Sister was out of it because of the operations.

The day after, she was lucid and told my mother what happened. Mom said back to her adamantly — "No, it didn't!" Mom was not willing to hear about his indiscretions. She had her Mormon fantasy of being with him in their afterlife, and so wasn't willing to have her daughter mess that up. No one ever asked any of the five of us what it did to us to lose our dad.

We then all moved to Utah. Somehow we got through that year. Then my mother decided to get rid of my sister and me by sending my sister back to North Carolina for her senior year and me to South Carolina for Military

School, where I was beaten.

The father of the family my sister was staying at put the moves on her, so my sister hooked up with a boyfriend. She called my mother to say she was going to get married. My mom jumped in right away with, "I'm getting married, too!" Mom took the joy away.

I hitchhiked up for the wedding, then went back south to Carlisle in order to finish up the school year. When school was out, the plan was for my sister's husband to go to basic training for the Air Force, so she and I were to spend three days on the train getting out to Utah to my mom's wedding. When we arrived at the station in Salt Lake City, my mom met us and held out her hand with a new ring on it saying, "We couldn't wait and got married yesterday!"

She then talked my newly married sister into watching us all summer while she went off to England with her new husband for her honeymoon. My sister didn't get a honeymoon. That summer, my next brother and I did a lot of criminal activity. We got caught and put in jail. Restitution was cleaning a school for months.

Mom still wouldn't talk about what had happened to my sister, who was like a lot of abused kids, still trying to get their parents approval even after the abuse. What can a daughter give her mother as the greatest gift? A year later, she called up my mother and says, "Mom, I'm pregnant!" My mother, without skipping a beat says, "I'm pregnant!" We joke about our mom having her own granddaughter.

And so it went. My sister was married to an unlovable man and produced two children. She drank and smoked heavily. Each year, once or twice, she tried to connect with Mom. To fortify herself, she would drink. Mom would detect she was drinking (against her Mormon values even though she herself had, even in Utah), be disgusted again, then criticize, and the conversation would deteriorate. I was in my late 20s when my sister told me what was really going on. The poor woman had still been keeping the secret like she'd been trained.

My mother's second marriage lasted seven years. I later found out he had severely beaten my two youngest brothers at times, especially the third one down. That brother eventually OD'd on heroin as an adult while on a cot in a homeless shelter in Seattle.

Mom married another guy and then had it annulled after two years. She took back my dad's name, as she longed to be with him in heaven.

A few years later, my sister finally divorced her neglectful and verbally dismissive husband, and then married an ex-policeman. He ended up adding physical abuse to the mix. She continued to deteriorate, but still was periodically trying to get mom's acceptance.

With the family problems we were immersed in, and her being saddled with us four brothers, my sister was frustrated a lot growing up. I was particularly difficult, and she called me stupid throughout my childhood. We had an uneasy relationship as she was BPD (Borderline Personality Disorder) from all of the abandonment and abuse, and it was hard to trust she wouldn't hurt me. When I took my new wife out to California to meet her for the first time, I was 30, and we went to a restaurant up on the hills of Palo Alto, California. She drank her wine and brashly talked, reminiscing about family foibles. I stayed a bit reserved in order to not flinch at her barbs and zingers.

We said our goodbyes and I drove down Sand Hill Road, headed to the Stanford shopping center.

My wife said, "I cant believe how much she needs your approval."

"What?" I replied. "She was cutting and digging almost the whole time."

She said, "Run the movie."

I visualized the conversation we'd just had, only I jumped to the mental camera-three position of objectivity. BAM — I saw it. It hit me like a ton of bricks. I had to pull over because I was sobbing so hard. That poor woman. My poor sister. She was SO needy and desperate. I'd gotten out of my crap and was able to see her pain, then feel it. From that moment on, I never criticized her and gave her whatever I could to make her feel better.

She still could hurt me with things she said, because she didn't know what she was doing, but I didn't take it personally anymore.

A few years later, she escaped her second husband by hiding at her daughter's house in Kentucky. She gradually went downhill, continuing to drink and smoke. Then I got a call that she'd gone into the hospital. I bought an airline ticket to go see her. When I called to say I was coming out, she said to wait until she was home as it would be better when she could visit properly.

Two days later, she was gone. I'd missed the window.

What a waste we all suffered through because our parents wouldn't look at what they were doing to us. My dad's narcissism and my mother's histrionics crippled all five of their children's lives. We each suffered in our own way, but my sister took the brunt of it.

It set us all up for lives of searching for love and approval with the worst tools: fear, desperation, and shame. The three of us who survived still have the scars from it all. All three of us married women who were variations of our mother and eventually divorced them, going on to marry really wonderful people. But I grieve the other two whose lives were lost due to the selfishness of our "caregivers."

The ripples of abuse go on for generations. We, as well as our children, suffer when we don't get help. The secrets eat our souls.

Gloria Steinem - Steinem is a legend and a leader of the American feminist movement in the late 1960s and early 1970s. She continues her social activism today and is a journalist and author. She is a lecturer and feminist organizer throughout the world. Her first book published in more than 20 years, "My Life on the Road," explores her account as a writer and catalyst for change. She states, "The best way for us to cultivate fearlessness in our daughters and other young women is by example. If they see their mothers and other women in their lives going forward despite fear, they'll know it's possible."

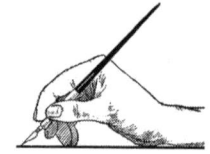

Renee, 48, Arizona, USA

I am a strong, independent, and educated woman.

I kept saying this to myself while I looked at one woman after another's depictions of their #MeToo experiences on social media. Little did I know that what I was thinking was completely antithetical to what really happened to me.

When I was 13, when I was 14, when I was 18, and yes, even when I was 30, all of these experiences came rushing back into my mind. Throughout these different times and experiences with men whom I both knew and didn't know, there was this feeling in the pit of my stomach that did not feel right. It did not feel as though I was attracted to this person. Or this person was someone I didn't want to disappoint or make angry. I now realize that feeling is one which many strong, independent, and even educated women ignore. Because the next rationalization is, "just let him/her get it over with."

I know now from many introspective activities, sessions with therapists, and more that a lot of my reactions were from my lack of self-worth. For me, that can be traced back to my father's suicide when I was 2 years old. But for others, it can be many types of traumas which influence our choices and shape our identities. This rationalization is the #MeToo paradigm shift with which I identify.

Why was I unable to simply say "no" when a 25-year-old man was fondling me at 13 years old? I was taught about sex at a young age, and my sister and I were raised as empowered little girls by a strong, independent single mother. We were taught about inappropriate touching and sexual abuse, how babies were made, and the functions of the human body.

So, why did I just sit there while this man pulled down my shorts and touched my vagina? I didn't make a sound. I thought about how I must seem really "grown up" for this man to be attracted to me. I mean, I had always had a crush on him. But he was just one of the experiences during this period until we moved away when I was 16. I just kept remembering how I was so grown up.

Some of the experiences which happened when I was older were more violent and unwanted. Why did I rationalize that I was being assaulted or raped rather than THEY were the ones assaulting and raping ME? Only now do I understand that this is a societal issue/problem and not MINE.

At 27 years old, my boyfriend and I were sexually active and monogamous. One morning, I woke up to him touching me. I was sleeping on my stomach, and he climbed behind me and pressed himself into me several times. Then he pinned my arms down and entered my anus.

Even after saying, "NO!" to anal sex in the past, he held me down even while I screamed in pain as he entered me over and over. My roommate heard me and stormed in and stopped what could have been so much worse.

And that was my rationalization: "it could have been worse," After all, I am a strong, independent, educated woman, so this doesn't happen to me. I made the choice to continue these acts, right? I must have asked for it, I sent off the wrong signals and don't want to be seen as a tease.

Now, I finally understand I was seeing these acts as a type of "medication" to soothe the wounds of low self-worth. If I convinced myself that it was my fault and I chose this, then I would only need to forgive one person -- ME. This empowers me, or so I thought.

But it doesn't. What it does is give those who behaved badly a "pass" by not holding THEM accountable for THEIR assaults and actions.

Now it is time. I am a strong, independent, powerful, and educated woman.

And #MeToo.

Apolonia, 31, Florida, USA

Permission Unnecessary

When discussing sexual harassment and assault, where does one start? What is the beginning? The first time it happened? The first time you realize it was happening? Or the most recent time it happened?

Sexual harassment is so prevalent it's hard to even categorize these encounters. It's hard to admit they happened and it's hard to talk about. It's even harder when you're made to feel like it's your fault or you could have prevented it.

My first encounter or memory of it, was my female cousin being molested by our step-grandfather when we were both extremely young. No one believed her when she finally told her story. I could have corroborated, but I was even younger than her and didn't understand what was happening. I didn't endure as much as she did because my home life was more stable, and my mother was protective and had endured being molested growing up as well, so she kept a close eye on me. Unfortunately, not close enough.

I watched everyone tear apart my cousin's life and credibility because there was no way this hard-working man, who also worked for the school board, could be such a monster. It must be her emotional issues and need for attention coming out. They blamed a child and called her a liar. Why would I put myself through that, too? My cousin was passed around from family member to family member because her mother was unfit, and now she was no longer welcome at my grandmother's home. She eventually went back to my grandparents as a last resort and she had to swear she "wouldn't cause trouble."

The truth eventually came to light, for my cousin, at least. To this day, that situation makes me feel disgusted and angry. Mainly with myself.

But isn't that how we're programmed? I could've said something; I could've done something. The monster is within; the man has no control over himself, so it must be us. A child was made to blame herself.

Later, in middle school, a friend's older boyfriend laid on top of me until I threatened to scream and tell my friend. He thought it was funny and kept trying to kiss me despite my repeated attempts to push him off and away. I'll never forget the feeling of panic that started to take over, and the hatred I felt when he got angry that I was crying.

In high school, my boobs were grabbed on a frequent basis, my bra strap was snapped, and guys old and young alike would constantly walk "by accident" into the girls dressing rooms when I was in drama/musical theater.

At this point, I think I started to feel numb and accept that this is just how life is. Nobody cares what I want and no one cares what I'm comfortable with.

My first sexual encounter was when I was about 17 and the guy was approximately 24. It wasn't planned on my part, but I was left alone with him drunk at the end of a long night of partying. It wasn't rape because I didn't dare to say no, but it also wasn't wanted. He definitely made it clear I wasn't welcome to stay at his house otherwise, and I'd been left without a car and didn't have a cell phone at the time.

Over the years, our group of friends realized he had a thing for younger girls, and eventually someone did accuse him of rape. Nothing ever came of it, and years later I would still see him around town.

During college, there were many instances of unwanted advances. Whether it was being groped in a crowded bar with no escape, unsolicited dick pics, or waking up once at home and once at the hospital after getting drugged.

The first time it happened, I had luckily been with a group of friends who were able to get me home when I started to get unresponsive. It's the same story: "You were fine one second, and in an instant it was like you were blackout drunk."

The second time I was at a bar I frequented with bartenders I wouldn't call friends, but who knew my name and drink order. Luckily for me, they called an ambulance and wouldn't let a guy take me home -- to this day, I have no clue who that guy was. I had come in with work friends and stayed to finish my drink when they left. It should have only been a 30-minute difference and the usual quick walk to my apartment. Instead, it resulted in me waking up in a hospital bed being watched by an old man security guard who refused to let me leave until the doctor said I could go.

I think it's safe to say, every instance had to do with someone exerting their dominance and feeling of entitlement on me. I wish I could say this ended in college. I wish I could say when I reached my 30s I didn't have to worry about any of that stuff again.

At 31, I woke up in a hospital with sexual assault listed in my medical records. Even now, the details escape me, but I had to take a cab home from the hospital in a gown and jeans because my top had been ripped apart. I had to pay for that hospital visit. I had to pay for what someone else did to me. I had to endure a female nurse badgering me for details, getting misty eyed and hugging me before letting me check myself out. A hug was the last thing that I wanted. I wanted to go home and pretend nothing happened. It was easier to do nothing than to accept what happened and answer any more questions.

This is what I do every time. Denial and acceptance are very different, but both seem to get the job done.

I'm angry. All of this makes me angry. I'm angry this is not a unique story. I'm angry anyone has had to endure this bullshit. I'm angry I'm not an exception to the rule and this behavior is so prevalent. I'm angry I've never spoken up and I'm angry I've never been able to hold anyone accountable for their behavior.

I'm angry and disgusted that each time these things have happened, I've wondered what I could do differently. I'm angry I let someone else take control of me physically, mentally, and emotionally. I'm angry I've made and laughed at rape jokes. I'm angry my ex-boyfriend laughed when I would get dick pics from other guys. I'm angry that the only way some people can get off is by hurting others. I'm angry there is no accountability. I'm angry we all have to share the humiliating and intimate details of our lives to get anyone to listen or care.

I'm angry I've seen so many men think #metoo is a feminist movement or something to laugh at. I'm angry that it's not. I'm angry that it's real and this is life for so many people, female and male.

More than anger, though, I feel relief and I feel hope.

I feel relief that strong people from every walk of life are coming together to address these issues. I feel hope we can change society and improve the lives for those who come after us. I feel hope for accountability and not sweeping everything under the rug from now on. I feel hope of preventing further moments of terror, demeaning, depression, hate, and anger.

Hannah Wilke - 1940-1993 - Wilke was an American painter, sculptor, photographer, video artist, and performance artist. Her work explores the issues of feminism, femininity, and sexuality and has been exhibited throughout the world. During her life, Wilke was widely exhibited, and although controversial, received critical praise. She and other feminist artists of their time used confrontational female sexuality, making them difficult to appeal to the patriarchy of the museum culture. However, since her death, Wilke's work has been added to many permanent collections such as The Museum of Modern Art, the Whitney Museum of American Art, Los Angeles County Museum of Art, Museum of Contemporary Art in Los Angeles, and in the Centre Pompidou in Paris.

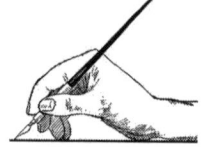

Carolyn M., Toronto, Canada

When I was in my early 20s, I worked as a buyer's agent for a real estate agent at a large real estate company. The agent, Roger, was the brother of my father's best friend and had known me since childhood.

This is what it was like to work for that man:

• Multiple times a day he would ask me if my "pussy was dripping" or when I was going to show him my breasts, "just a peek," he would say.
• Before he left for his cottage in Muskoka on Lake Joe, he would tell me I could bring my boyfriend to the office and should have sex in the office on the weekends when the administrative assistant wasn't there. (The agent and his team work from his home office). I would often find myself scanning the walls and shelves, convinced there were cameras.
• He found sick pleasure in taking a big shit in his private washroom, which was attached to his private office, leaving the door open and then inviting me in for a meeting, forcing me to sit in his stench, which took over the small room.
• He would have me accompany him to "meetings" with friends with lots of alcohol and then suggest that I hook up with them.
• When I got to the office one morning, he and his wife were in his office. They asked me to come into his office because they had something they wanted to discuss with me. The evening before, he had interviewed a woman for an administrative assistant position he was hiring for, and after the interview, his wife offered the interviewee a ride home. In the car, the woman told her that during the interview Roger had gone into great detail to describe my body, specifically my large breasts. The way he spoke about me made the woman feel very uncomfortable and she felt his wife should know and was obviously not taking the job. Roger told both myself and his wife that he never said that, the woman had made that up. Really?!

How can a woman who had never met me "make up" that description?
- I was in Thailand during the devastating 2004 tsunami, and once I was back, the agent would yell, "TSUNAMI!" in the office, even after I asked him to stop and explained (fighting back tears) that it was an emotional experience for me.
- He changed all my passwords and blocked my access to his network after I confided in his wife about how, when my boyfriend came home in a drug- and alcohol-fueled state while I was sleeping, he threw milk pitchers full of water on me to wake me up. A fight followed, after which I required medical attention and my boyfriend was arrested. He would later be arrested again after violating his restraining order.
- The agent still owes me money for administrative work I did for him.
- I never worked in real estate again after that. As I'm writing this, I'm realizing that at the time it was easier for me to walk away from money and a career in an entire industry than it was for me to walk away from the sexual harassment I endured during the year and a half or so that I worked for that agent.

Helen Reddy – Reddy is an Australian pop singer who won the first American Music Award for 'Favorite Pop/Rock Female Artist' with her song "I am Woman," which then became an anthem for the second-wave of feminism and she was made into a feminist icon.

Monet, 35, New York, USA

Before there was a #metoo or #timesup movement, like others, there was me. I am finally taking a stand to say "no more!"

I remember vividly the first time I was sexually harassed. It was in Trinidad, where I was born. I was only 12 or 13 years old. My mother sent me to the supermarket, which was a short walk from our home, and a man who must have been in his 20s was catcalling me. Being the brave and bold little "hot mouth" I was, I wanted to put him in his place. I shouted at him from the other side of the street asking if something was stuck in his teeth. Well, can I just tell you, the shame I felt across my being when he responded "Yes! Salt fish!" was enough to make me hide for days.

Years and years of catcalls later, spanning from Trinidad across the ocean to America, I would still feel the heat of shame and disgust whenever I sensed the eyes of strange men on the subways undressing me or saying things in their native languages that wreaked of profanity. Everyone around me could sense it, too.

Unfortunately, catcalls turned to more; my worst experience with harassment was in the workplace. This harassment in some ways echoed allegations from others around the world about powerful men. It was harassment I had to endure because I had bills to pay. But then I became a mom and I guess along with gaining a precious little girl, I also grew some serious courage, because I finally used that courage to take a stand. To rise up, not just for myself, but for my daughter and any other person who would suffer the narcissistic audacity of those who seem to believe that a person's body is an invitation to be sexually inappropriate, either physically or verbally, whether with lewd comments or violent molestation.

Being violated in such a way really affected me. Having to face the insult, shame and uncertainties along with the emotional and psychological issues from which being a perpetrator's target brings.
Every day is a challenge because there are days when I feel powerful and

empowered, but then there are days when I just feel angry and frustrated.
- Frustrated at the idea that a man or woman would think lewd and disgusting acts of assault and violence would be welcomed.
- Frustrated at constantly wondering what goes on in a person's mind to make him/her not consider the effects of their actions on others.
- Frustrated the "highfalutin'" friends and acquaintances of these culprits are more than happy to feign ignorance and complacency or simply make excuses for a perpetrator's attitude and misbehavior. I don't think I ever want to hear the phrase "boys will be boys" again.
- Frustrated by tactics which border on stalking a victim's friend or family members, or to grasp at straws, search, obtain and use private moments out of context in an effort to defend one's illegal and immoral actions, knowing all too well they are tormenting us. In addition to denying their misbehavior, they try to accuse us for it happening and continue to persecute us for it, using it to victimize us over and over again. That it is allowed as a defense to take the private lives, self-confidence, strength, and the enjoyment of our freedom and liberties, and use it against us to call us "instigators."
- Frustrated the narcissists of this world can continue go to great lengths to protect themselves by continuing to abuse their power and influence after subjecting others to unwanted lewd and obscene behavior that in their minds is somehow warranted.
- Frustrated that as in a country where we proudly proclaim ourselves to be "home of the free," I am subjected to unwanted sexual advances.
- Frustrated with the fact that all of these actions can result in losing jobs, losing friends and colleagues when you try to stand up for yourself and fight back.

But through the frustration, I find it necessary to look at the positive and be in a state of gratitude.

While I am grateful that my story is not as serious as others, I imagine everyone affected by any form of sexual assault has their lives ruined in different ways, which is unforgivable.

Through my anger, I always have to remind myself I can either be an angry, resentful, bitter ball of nothingness, or I can look at the good which has come from being sexually harassed.

Understanding resistance and resolving problems by not condemning them has helped me to find the positive in being a target of sexual harassment, which for me is:

- I was brave!
- I found out who the good people in my life were while learning a valuable lesson on trust and loyalty. Their constant support and encouragement made me feel like I could move mountains.
- I discovered my strength. I never knew what a force I am and how fearless I can be.
- I am a good egg. And a selfless person.

"When I change the way I look at things, the things I look at change." -- Dr. Wayne Dyer

No one asks to be harassed or discriminated against. No one deserves in any manner to be discriminated against or harassed, and to insinuate that because someone is free-spirited in their personal life is an invitation or reason for harassment is like saying a stripper somehow desires to be raped. What society are we living in? Is this America or the Middle East? Where has the humane in humanity gone? Where is the simple common decency of respect for others and where is the compassion?

With empowerment comes expense. Financial, economic, psychological, and social expense. Standing up for yourself, standing up for what is right, can change your life.

Two years later and my future is still uncertain and might be for some time. What is certain is I am determined to make every day better than the last, not just for me, but for my daughter and for anyone who is going through their own struggles as a result of sexual harassment and violence.

Unfortunately, the war on respect for women still ensues.

What gives someone the idea that acting sexually inappropriate toward another person is okay? Are we truly this astonished that it keeps happening or are people just taken aback that women have finally had enough and now have the balls to stand up, and not just fight back, but fight back harder and openly regardless of the consequences?

In the midst of questioning and criticizing the motives of famous women heading the #Metoo and #Timesup movement, let's not lose sight of the meaning and reasons as to why the floodgates have opened.

What matters now is that we have created a movement of what I want to call "encouragement," rather than empowerment. To send the message there are those of us who are standing with each other for each other.

Because let's not pretend there aren't people who purposely and maliciously stand by and allow sexual assault to happen. The good women of the world are sending the message to women such as myself, who was able to stand up to my predators and shake them down, that we are not to blame, we are not to be ashamed.

Women have fought for the right of equality and the right to vote. Now, we demand the right of respect for our bodies. If we as a society continue to allow sexual misconduct, abuse and harassment to continue, then in essence, we are the same as so many other cultures and societies who suppress their women.

I hope to use my experiences to be productive and useful, to be a part of educating and bringing awareness of this social and criminal hazard to others, and help show them how to fight against it, and put an end to it once and for all.

John Stoltenberg – *In 1989, Stoltenberg founded a group called "Men Can Stop Rape," which examined the need for men to seek and embrace a version of masculinity which is less toxic and based upon respect rather than misogyny. He also studied pornography, concentrating on its effects on men's sexuality in the dominance, objectification, and dehumanization of women. He is married to feminist writer Andrea Dworkin.*

Carol R. T., 70, Kentucky, USA

#MeToo.

At age 18, just out of high school and leading a sheltered life, I joined the U.S. Air Force. From 1965 to 1968, I was sexually harassed by a training instructor. I didn't speak out because I didn't realize I could, and I was afraid of what would happen to me. I was not in a position of power and authority as he was. It was a scary time. I would go nowhere on base by myself. I made sure a friend or two was always with me, since he would follow me around.

Long story, but all too common. I've seen women speak out in other jobs I've held, and I've seen how they were harassed so badly by authority figures and by those whom they spoke out against that they had to quit a job they loved in order to have peace.

Women pay a big price for speaking up. That's why many wait or never speak out at all.

\#

Hillary Rodham Clinton - "I believe the rights of women and girls is the unfinished business of the 21st Century." Clinton has hit many firsts in her lifetime. In 1993, President Bill Clinton appointed Hillary to chair a Task Force on National Health Care Reform and was a major force behind the passage of the State Children's Health Insurance Program (CHIP) in 1997. She helped create the Office on Violence Against Women at the Department of Justice, and initiated the Adoption and Safe Families Act, which she regards her greatest accomplishment as first lady. Clinton led the "No Ceilings: The Full Participation Project" in partnership with the Bill & Melinda Gates Foundation. In 2000, she was the first First Lady to march in an LGBT pride parade and served as state senator of New York. Clinton has heavily focused on women and family issues and supports universal preschool. She served as secretary of state to President Barack Obama and was formally nominated at the 2016 Democratic National Convention in Philadelphia on July 26, 2016, becoming the first woman to be nominated for president by a major U.S. political party.

Kee, 19, California, USA

October

That week in October, I didn't know my life would be changed forever. I couldn't know.

You hear so many people give you spiels about how to prevent it, but no one truly understands. How could they? No one has experienced anything like this before. Doesn't everyone respond differently? So, how should I know what weapon to choose during this fight? Engulfed in the immense amount of sensations from the drugs, I know it's wrong but you can't really blame me. You cannot advocate for what you do not know, so this fuel and this fire can't be put out with a bucket of tears.

That week in October, I had so much planned for myself, with it being my first month of being 18 years old. Yet, I couldn't know the memories I expected to make would be overshadowed by one nightmare.
On this day, I had dreams of being alone. No parents, just friends and our running imaginations. But come nightfall, the evils were lurking.

Everyone has their own demons. You just have to make sure you don't nurse them. My demon was an 11-year-old girl, trapped in the misery of her own beliefs and bullying. Beliefs that she was worthless. Bullied by other people's insecurities being projected onto her. But how they end up being demons: They are suppressed behind locked lips, withholding the key. Everyone knew this. They could see it in my shy, quivering hands. I hate to break it to you, but that's how you put a target on yourself. I did not realize it would change my life that night with the person whom I trusted the most. My uncle, who I had dreamt of walking me down the aisle.

It wasn't even the crime that tore me down the most. Every drunken attempt to seduce his own flesh and blood made me infuriated. I did not realize at the time he was setting me up for slaughter. He was a very manipulative man who inspired love in me before the bond was so quickly broken. October 29th, 2016, at 11:00 p.m. He was supposed to check up on me that day. Everything was right. I accepted his call with open arms and he greeted me with love, or so I thought. Taunting me (which I now know) with the line that he was my only connection to my biological father, who had died when I was 2. All I had to rely on were the stories people would tell. My uncle used these stories to make me trust him and explained how he would love and protect me. Funny how I can remember him being the one to tell me how to save myself from danger. From rape.

About 20 minutes passed, his speech slurring with every promise. The last promise he made was to feed the start of my own unhealthy addiction to smoking weed. Being an experimental teen, I agreed immediately. He even offered a bed to stay the night, which wasn't unusual. He was a family man, which definitely makes sense to me now. He connected with each of our broken souls, having easier access to his deepest, darkest desires. Though he is a felon, no one could imagine a family member could commit such a heinous act. A brother, a father, a son, a cousin, a nephew, an uncle. Not to his own flesh and blood.

He constantly called me, pushing me to sneak past the family home's new camera systems. There was one at the doorbell and one peering down on the entrance of the home. One in the corner of the living room, so you are able to see all the way to the kitchen. The last camera was set up to view the backyard, but not the sides of the house. So, when he called me, he told me to take the opportunity of sneaking out of the garage door.

I grabbed my own stash of weed and some undergarments to put in my purse for the next day. I didn't want to seem suspicious with a backpack, so I was relying on him for pajamas. I made my way to the laundry room and out the door, leaving the alarm system off so it wouldn't alert my parents, who were leaving soon to go on their annual cruise.

When I made it to the side of the house, I jumped in the bushes, diving into the neighbor's yard. Out of sight of the garage camera, I ran along the neighbor's yard and circled around the corner to keep out of sight. When I reached my car, which was parked across the street from the house, I made a U-turn to further hide the evidence of my disappearance.

It's funny, because I now realize my parents didn't even pay close attention to the tapes and rewind them back, though I really wish they had that night. But at the time, I was fed up with being under constant surveillance, and once again he gave me a place in which I felt understood. I wanted to be a rebel that night because he made me feel liberated and free, something I was not used to feeling. Like a normal teenager, I was wanting to be an adult my whole young life. I waited 18 years for this! 18 years and 29 days to be exact.

I began to get annoyed with the constant calls and him asking, "Where are you?" "Did you make it out?" "How far are you?" But it did make me feel secure that someone would talk and be with me the whole way. He texted me the address, the only thing he couldn't speak through the phone. He wanted to keep most communication through phone calls, so he wouldn't be traced or have anyone read over the details of our meet up. Now that common sense has come back to me, I realize it made absolutely no sense. But then again, that's how much I trusted him at the time.

I was feeling confident in my decision until I was about 15 minutes away from his home. He was asking personal questions about my sexual orientation, my virginity, and the type of underwear I was wearing. But he was a drunken mess as always, and he knew how to insert jokes into the conversation, so maybe he was joking. He was the life of the party, and I couldn't differentiate that from my own boundaries. Deep down I knew it was odd and uncomfortable, so I just laughed it off.

When I was close to my fate, he finally told me that no one else was home. The eldest was off with her partner and the wife had left was the kids. I really wanted to turn back around then and there, but it was so late to drive such a long way back. I had little gas and no money to be trying to find my way back home, and I would even get to work earlier because I was so much closer. I figured I'd just spend the night with no problems. I mean he was my uncle, for Christ's sake, I thought I was tripping.

When I arrived, he was waiting on the patio with no shirt on and a bottle of alcohol in one hand. My nerves started to rise when I saw it was completely dark and he had me pull my car in the driveway on the side of the house. I grabbed my belongings and the small nugs of marijuana I had and got out of my car. He seemed very anxious himself, constantly looking down the empty street and rushing me inside. It was even more eerie once I got inside. There were no lights and a few pieces of furniture and clothes spread around, for they had recently moved into the new house.

He took me upstairs to the master bedroom and let me hop in his shower and get into the pajamas he supplied. Once I was in the shower and was washing up, he slid open the glass door to the shower and peered inside. I completely froze and every bone in my body was completely stiff. Feeling completely vulnerable, I began to feel myself shrink inside and out. It was as if time had gone slow.

I got out and slipped on the clothing with the intention of leaving. He was nowhere to be found, then all of a sudden, he appeared in the room and removed his boxer shorts, sending me further down the abyss of my soul and making the sweat trickle from my forehead.

Then it began to make sense, so crisp and so clear. What he whispered before, "You're cool, I know you can keep a secret." It wasn't the drugs, it was about something much more sinister. More purposefully unclear statements about how we were both adults and the "fun" should be kept between us.

He pulled me close and made me take off the clothing I had put on. I completely submitted out of terror and the fact that he was triple my size and weight. The worst part was not the rape, it was not the part about me being dragged across the house and unable to push a man whom I had loved so dearly off of me.

The worst part was the kisses he thought would be so intimate and genuine. It was then that I realized time had gotten even slower. All I could think about was getting out of there. I was looking over my shoulder at his family photos and wondering how disappointed they would be if I dared to open my mouth. That was the first lie I told myself, then and there. Once it was over, he laid his large arm over me while he slept, and I shakingly got up to take the money from his wallet for toll bridge to get back home.

I was completely distraught and panicking once I was alone in the car and trying to find my way home. I cried that night and every night after, but I survived, which is what I should have been reminding myself the truth of from the beginning.

I went to work and school the next day, and acted like everything was normal. I did this for one whole year, even after he moved down the street from me and would invite himself over to family functions. I suppose I pushed the memory and feelings so deep down that I had almost forgotten them.

I never had the chance to face my feelings about the situation until I went into complete panic-mode on the anniversary week a year later. It had driven me so mad I had to be detained in a mental facility for a week. It helped me come face-to-face with my PTSD and depression, and I found solitude in my hospital's individual and group therapy sessions. I could relate to other people and be able to talk about it so freely. With coming out with my story, I had allowed several other family members to come forward about the same exact man. I had purged myself of the sorrow and the anger portion of the assault and was ready for the healing portion, within myself and others.

Though I have much work to do and many legal battles to face, among other fallout, I am glad to share my story and I would not wish to change the steps I have taken. It has given me character and the voice to help others. Sexual assault is a serious topic and no person should feel as though it should be kept to themselves, no matter the circumstance or person. Whether it is a male, female, young, old, stranger, friend, or family member, they shall be held accountable.

There is this one impactful photo I recently saw on Twitter, which outlines the negative aspects of assault culture in a pyramid diagram. At the bottom is Victimization, which includes victim-blaming, "jokes," "locker room talk," non-consensual photography, and excuses such as "boys will be boys." The next step up the pyramid is Degradation. This is cat-calling, unwanted nude or clothed photos, threats and stalking, and revenge porn. Leaning into assault is the Removal of Autonomy. In this section, it includes groping, dosing, sexual coercion, safe word violations, condom removal, molestation, and statutory rape. Lastly, the most triggering is Explicit Violence: rape, incest, battery, and murder. These are all important issues which should absolutely be taken seriously anywhere.

No matter how small or large anyone believes they are, it is very much equally damaging. The "smaller" things such as cat-calling or unwanted photos taken of a person can definitely be triggering as well as a violation of a basic human right. To stop these vicious cycles, we have to start with ourselves.

Knowing and understanding the various acts of assault and correcting them with what you see in everyday life is a beginning. Being able to stop your close ones from doing such things can have a major impact, because it always starts with one. Then graduating to speaking to strangers and through organizations and such. But speaking up should not be limited to people who have already done wrong; speak to your children, teach them what's right and wrong to and from others.

Please be able to communicate and have an effective relationship because they might have struggled with the same predicament and are simply projecting these horrendous crimes. The time to end this incredible traumatizing is past overdue.

I am thankful for Jyssica for making this book to highlight the danger of assault in its many forms. I know we can start a revolution and help many victims struggling with their past. We can also help by sharing warning signs about how you can try to stop an assault before it happens. You have a right to be in a safe place. Thank you.

John Stuart Mill & Harriet Taylor Mill – *In 1866, J.S. Mill became the first member of British Parliament to promote the women's vote by introducing the first bill in Britain calling for suffrage. He and his wife wrote "The Subjection of Women" in 1861. They talked about the role of women in marriage and how it needed to be changed, commenting on three major facets of women's lives they felt were hindering women: society and gender construction, education, and marriage. The Mills argued that the oppression of women was a remaining relic from ancient times, which included a set of prejudices which severely impeded the progress of humanity.*

Crystal, 43, Ohio, USA

I was sexually abused from ages 3 to 13 by my two uncles. Every weekend and every summer. Both of my uncles were what I call "typical abusers" because they used attention and time to get the sex they wanted. It started when I was 3 years old in the bathtub with just fondling and digital penetration.

My mom found the neighbor on top of me at age 5.

When I was 9, my stepbrother moved in and severe physical abuse started.

At 11, I was kidnapped by my mom and taken to Montana. It took three months to get there. My stepbrother started brutal rape and torture. I was tied up in the mountains for hours. We were homesteading.

My stepbrother was a brutal sadist. He raped and beat me with anything around. Bottles, sticks, himself, knives, the dog. He killed every animal I ever got close to. Most days I thought he would kill me, too. He would tie me up in the woods for hours, and when he was done, he would leave me there. I became very suicidal after his abuse. I was going to kill myself.

My dad eventually found us and kidnapped me back. Then back home with him, my uncles started abusing me again.

I dated a security guard from school. He was 47 and I was 15. I needed protection from my stepbrother, since he was back in the house. I was institutionalized during my teens for suicide attempts. At one point, I dated a teacher. He was 64, I was 16 and living in a group home.

I spent most of my teenage years in institutions to keep me from committing suicide. That's when I disclosed the abuse. My family didn't believe me and I was called a liar. My stepmother broke my nose for "ruining my uncle's marriage."

I married on the day I turned 18, just to get out of my dad's house, as Dad's emotional abuse was awful, and, of course, there was the stepmother and stepbrother in the home. My new husband was 47 years old. I left that marriage a year later, as my husband was very physically abusive and jealous. I left and went right to an alcoholic, whom I stayed with for two years. We were engaged, but he raped me several times, and even tied me to the bed on different occasions. He choked me.

I finally left him and became a stripper to put myself through school. Then, I met a great guy. who was 46 years older than me. We got married after several years. Unfortunately, he was addicted to prescription painkillers and I just couldn't deal with it.

I later got into horses. They saved me, along with several guardian angels who won't let me go, for some reason.

This is the main gist of my life of abuse. My stepbrother is a monster. My uncles were your "typical molesters."

It has ended, but all of the abuse has affected me and my body and my health. At 24, I was diagnosed with cervical cancer. One of my abusers had HPV and he gave it to me. I had to have a total hysterectomy because of it. That tore me up and I went through it alone.

Today, I still deal with the effects of the abuse. I'm back in counseling. I was doing really well with the help of my horse before I got sick again. These last five years have been very trying. My entire digestive system shut down. I had to have seven surgeries in 20 months, which threw me for a loop. The scars brought back everything my stepbrother did to me. Those same scars.

I have branched out to expressive arts, EMDR, mindfulness, and talk therapy. It has helped, but the depression gets the best of me sometimes. I fight every single day to wake up and go through the day; sometimes I would rather not. My body is riddled with pain from malnutrition, neuropathy, myalgia. The illness and the past like to intertwine themselves to feed each other. I try not to let it get too bad. Most days I succeed; others not so well. I still manage to make it to the next day, though.

My legacy of abuse stops with me. Hopefully, the cycle does, too.

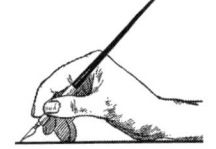

Bob, 62, New York, USA
Damaged Goods

I wasn't sure where to start, but it needs to be early.

I am the youngest of three children. My sister was four years older and my brother was five years older than me. My guess is that I was the save-the-marriage baby.

One of my earliest childhood memories was when I tossed my brother's and sister's Easter bunnies down the cellar stairs. I remember looking down the dark passage knowing I did something wrong. I wasn't an animal killer because the next time I maimed anything was when I killed a goldfinch with a BB gun, and I felt so bad I vowed I would never do it again.

When I was 5 years old, I started having some frightening dreams, but I couldn't wait to go to bed because I had found the ability to levitate out of my body while still awake. I would just lie still and calmly levitate to the ceiling and it was as if there were clouds around me. This went on for a few weeks, and eventually I could no longer do this. I tried to tell friends at school, thinking it was normal, but apparently not, because I was laughed at and ridiculed.

I had a friend named Benny, and we were inseparable and attended a Catholic school. We had to wear white shirts and green ties and always seemed to be in trouble. One day, I met up with Benny and he said he had something to show me. We went into a crawl space in an unfinished basement where he pulled out some stag magazines which belonged to his father.

Then things got weird and Benny wanted to try oral sex on me. I felt strange, but I allowed him to do it, and it happened a few more times before I said we should not do that anymore. It was something I never shared with anyone, but we stayed friends. By the third grade, I was failing in school, which for some reason meant I had to go across the street to a different elementary school to repeat third grade.

I had a habit of getting into fights, something which would follow me for a long time. And by the fifth grade, I had a growing interest in girls. My first two girlfriends were both named Roxanne, strangely enough. Roxanne the First was the one I kissed and did some touching, but nothing more. By this time, my father, a strict Korean War veteran who was never around much, had disappeared after we moved for the fifth time.

At the age of 12, a friend's sister, Sherry, said she had something for me and told me to meet her at the cemetery. She was 21. I rode my bike to the cemetery to meet her, and she had a blanket laid on the ground. Before long I had lost my virginity. After we were finished, I rode away much quicker than I did going to meet her.

During that same year, I got my next girlfriend, Roxanne the Second. She was a tomboy, a redhead, kind of loud and boisterous, and could play sports as well as some of the boys. We played down by the river a lot and other than some kissing, nothing really happened between us.

One day, my brother and a friend coaxed us into the backseat of an old car and made us strip. I remember sitting there feeling ashamed and embarrassed. I have never mentioned this to anyone ever until now at the age of 62; it's something I will carry to my grave.

When I entered junior high, it was grades seven to nine and a much larger school. I had earned the reputation of being the toughest guy at my elementary school, but this was a whole new ball game, and the fights came early and often. The problem was the other boys in my class didn't like me at all because of the fact I had no fear of girls, and many of them had never even kissed a girl, let alone gone round the bases, so I was seen as some kind of threat.

As I grew into my teens and in high school, I was having sex with anyone I could talk into it. Then I met my high school sweetheart, probably the only girl I truly loved. The sad part was that I cheated more than once. She was sweet, a cheerleader, and popular girl.
Even through two marriages, there was cheating on my part. In my young-

er days, I would masturbate before I went out to the bars so I wouldn't have that little devil on my shoulder, but he was always there.

Getting into my mid-40s, I still was dating here, and there but not settling down until I met Christine. She was a party girl built like a playboy bunny. I'd seen her out before, and one time she just came up and dragged me to the dance floor. Eventually my best friend brought her to the bar I went to after work. I am sitting there and someone came up behind me and covered my eyes, and when she took her hands away, behind me was Christine. She went home with me that night and we ended up living together.

We moved from upstate New York to Richmond, Virginia. We had a child, and then only three months after my daughter was born, Christine wanted out. I had already bought her a diamond ring, and I actually got on my knees saying we shouldn't break up and how we both came from broken homes. It didn't work and I kept my promise to move her home if she wasn't happy in Richmond.

Things really went downhill. I was stuck with a condo and a job, but I couldn't get out right away because I was in court trying to get custody of my daughter back from Christine, since she was off partying and doing drugs. I was going crazy and drinking like a fish. I had my first child at the age of 44, and I loved my daughter and Christine so much, I even helped her through rehab.

One afternoon, I was drinking and smoking, and was lonely, and I happened to be masturbating. There was a ruckus in the stairwell of the condo building. Stupid me, I was just staring out the window while still masturbating, just to see what was going on, not thinking anyone would see me. I see these three girls around my truck, and realized it was the paper carriers. All of a sudden, one of the girls points up at me. I am not sure how long I stood there, but it was definitely too long.

I knew this was not good. Here I was with all my ducks in a row to take full custody of my child, with all of my money tied up in babysitters and the court case. Nothing came of it right away, but about three months later, I was arrested. The way it went down was a bunch of lies; I am not trying to excuse my behavior, but there were things said which were simply not true. I plead out, but had to register as a level-one sex offender.

I was eventually able to pull myself back together financially and move back to New York. I had joint custody of my daughter and got my visitation rights squared away and I helped raise her until she was 11. We had a great bond. I held her in my arms when she was born, even before Christine did, and the first thought I had when holding her was "I won't ever let anyone hurt you."

When my daughter was 11, the whole thing came crashing down. I had registered in New York as a level-one sex offender, and the only thing they have is a zip code. One day, after many years, the clerk I normally spoke with was not at the desk when I went to re-register on the sex offender list. This time, it was a sheriff, and he told me I did not have to come there physically, I could actually take care of the paperwork by mail. He told me to wait there for five minutes, then told me I was "all set."

Two weeks later, I received a notice from the state with a long questionnaire form to fill out. I sent it back in and then I soon received a response letter stating that I was now a level-two sex offender and I had to go back to court.

This change ruined my life, and there was nothing I could do about it. I was out of money and I was advised to "not make any problems."

It wasn't long before Christine called me and told me to sign over custody of our girl or she would never let me see our daughter again. Like a fool, I didn't argue because I trusted this woman, though she and her mother really hated me by this point. Eventually, I got visitation with my daughter again, but I was not allowed to take her or be alone with her.

Then there started to be times when I would go to see her and Christine or her mother would send me away saying they made plans for her. Eventually, they stopped my visits altogether, and convinced my daughter she didn't need me in her life.

As of now, I have not seen my daughter in 10 years. No contact, no school pictures, and my dreams are crushed. Enough time has passed where it doesn't quite hurt as much, but there are still moments where the thought of never knowing her kills me.

I have not dated anyone in the past couple of years. I don't want it anymore. I mean, sure, I would love to have a companion to finish life with, but my heart is broken and it is difficult for me to trust anyone.

It has been quite some time, and all I can say is that it is hard growing up in a broken family and we have to let our children be children as a long as possible. I grew up very poor, but my mother was a saint and I have no idea how she did it for so many years alone.

It took me way too long to know what love actually is, and when you find it, hold onto it, don't let it go. Give them all the love you can so they don't end up as damaged goods. Don't make my mistakes.

Katharine Meyer "Kay" Graham - Graham was an American and the first female publisher of a major American newspaper. She led her family's newspaper, "The Washington Post," for more than two decades, overseeing its most famous period: the Watergate coverage which eventually led to the resignation of President Richard Nixon. Her memoir, "Personal History," won a Pulitzer Prize in 1998. She also became the first female Fortune 500 CEO in 1972, as CEO of the Washington Post company. As the only woman to be in such a high position at a publishing company, Graham had difficulty being taken seriously by many of her male colleagues and employees. She outlined in her memoir having a lack of confidence and not trusting in her own knowledge. The convergence of the women's movement with Graham's control of the Post brought about changes in her attitude and led her to promote gender equality within her company.

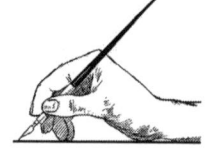

Linda, 58, Oklahoma, USA

Why would a woman wait for years to talk about sexual assault? For many reasons. This is my story.

When I went into the Air Force, it was the first time they blended flights (male and female). Toward the end of basic training, our flight was informed that a recruit and our drill sergeant had engaged in a sexual relationship. As a result, our flight was placed on administrative hold for a further month.

During that time, we were, as a group and individually, called whores, sluts, and worse by both men and women. I didn't even know what had occurred. During my last week in San Antonio, Texas, I was at the base club to hang out with friends, and a man kept asking me to dance. I politely said no, but he persisted. I was uncomfortable and decided to leave.

He grabbed my arm to pull me to the dance floor, called me a tease, and I punched him, knocking him into a giant fish tank which fell over. Gallons of water and fish went everywhere. I was the one banned from the club.

Later, at tech school, where there were only six women in my class, I had an instructor who would rub his parts up against me as I worked. If not for the intervention of a male student, I had no options. After what I saw happen in basic, I knew the repercussions of reporting would be humiliating.

The Roy Moore story and what's happening in Hollywood has brought up a lot of anger. My family was not supportive, they thought I either asked for it or I was too sensitive. I was told on more than one occasion that "that's what I get for trying to do a man's job."

I'm a strong woman and can hold my own. Times have changed. I have not talked about my experiences, but it doesn't mean they didn't happen. I'm 58 years old, retired from the military 17 years, and it still seems like yesterday.

\#

Madeleine Black, 52, Glasgow, Scotland

Editor's note: Madeleine Black is a counsellor and lives in Glasgow. Growing up in London in the late 1970s, she was brutally raped at the age of 13 by two American teenagers. In September 2014, after many years of keeping quiet and having come to terms with how the trauma had shaped her life, Madeleine decided to share her story publicly for the first time on The Forgiveness Project's website, and she completely underestimated the depth of the response to her story and vulnerability.

In her book "Unbroken" (2017), Madeleine tells her deeply moving and empowering story, as she discovers that life is about how she has chosen to recover from violence and adversity.

She has given permission to share some of her story in this book.

When I was 13, in a flat belonging to my friend's mother who was away for the weekend, I was attacked by two teenage American students. They held a knife to my throat and tortured, and raped me many times over, for four or five hours. I begged them to stop, but they just kicked me and laughed at me. I remember wishing they would kill me to make it all end.

During the event, I became aware of a young Tibetan monk in burgundy robes and an orange shawl by my right-hand side. I was also aware that I had floated out of my body and was on top of the wardrobe watching what was happening to me down below. The monk was praying next to my body, and telling me I was going to be okay. He covered up my naked body with his orange shawl and calmed me down.

Near the end, one of my attackers urinated on me, and out of everything they did, this felt like the worst, and it was one of the images which haunted me for years to come. Before they left, the more violent of the pair punched me in the chest, held the knife to my throat again, and said if I told anyone, he would find me and kill me. I believed him.

After that, I remember waking up with my friend in the bed next to me. I thought the noise of her bracelets were keys in the door, and I was worried that my attackers were coming back. I was covered in vomit, excrement, and blood.

We then spent the morning tidying up the flat and decided we shouldn't tell anyone, as we weren't meant to be there, and we had been drinking. It was now Sunday morning, and we went back to school the next day as if nothing had happened.

I lived in fear the two young men who had raped me would kill me one day. I felt worthless, totally degraded, and empty. I thought it was all my fault, and most of all I felt so dirty and contaminated. I would spend ages in the bath for many years afterward scrubbing my skin with cleaning products.

I started to become very promiscuous, as I had no self-respect. If a boy approached me, I just let him do whatever he wanted, because I thought if I resisted he would hurt me. At the same time, I started drinking and taking drugs. I stopped eating, as that was the only thing I felt I could control.

It became so painful to be alive that one night I took as many of my mum's pills as I could find, and ended up in a children's psychiatric ward, where I spent the next eight weeks. During that entire time, no one ever asked if anything had happened to me, even though I was clearly traumatized.

When I was about 16, I told my mum about the rape by writing down what had happened and leaving it on my pillow before I went to school one day.

My parents phoned my friend's mum, but my friend denied it all and said it had never happened like I said. My dad didn't believe her and wanted to go to the police, but I begged him not to, as I thought it was my fault and my attackers would come back and kill me. I couldn't believe what my friend had said.

I have often wondered what happened to my friend who was with me that night, and I have to accept that I honestly don't know. We had both been drinking heavily and she was put into another bedroom in the flat. It was the first time I had ever tried alcohol. The only outcomes I can assume are either she was also raped and blocked it out, or nothing happened to her and she passed out. When I reflect back to how she reacted when her mum was called by my parents, either scenario could fit.

I left school at 16 and my parents thought it would be good idea for me to get away, so when I was 17, I went to Israel for a year, where I worked on a kibbutz and in a town, which is where I met my husband.

I believe meeting him saved my life as I was on a path of self-destruction when I met him, but he loved me and made me feel worthwhile again. I used to drive him mad by constantly asking him why he loved me. When we talked about starting a family, I always told him I couldn't or didn't want children. In my head, I thought giving birth would be like being raped again.

After a while though, I decided I didn't want my rapists to take that part of my life away and I had to do this to heal myself. My revenge would be leading a good and happy life.

When my eldest daughter was nearly 13, I started to have a lot of flashbacks. I had nightmares for about three years, which would wake me up and I could feel the presence of the young men in the room, and at times could even feel their weight on my body. But the monk was always beside me, too.

Around this time, I was doing a psychotherapy course, and I knew it was finally time to talk about what had happened. I realised the only way to stop driving myself insane with all the memories that were flooding in was to come to terms with the rape, and accept it for what it was. After all, I had survived it and it wasn't happening anymore.

Most of my life, I hated the men who raped me, and wished them both a slow, painful death. However, as I was working with my therapist, something happened that I never set out to do: I chose to forgive them.

I used to think they were evil, but I started to understand that they didn't come into this world that way. They were born just like me, as an innocent baby. And then I started to wonder how they knew to be so violent and cruel to another human at such a young age. It made me think they couldn't have had the best of lives and had witnessed or experienced violence themselves.

I also realized they would never know if I felt hate toward them and the only person it was hurting was me. I can honestly say I have no fear, hate or revenge in my heart toward them anymore. I know that whatever they did to me, they can never touch the real essence of me and who I am. I am very lucky; I rebuilt my life, have a beautiful family and feel so grateful to be alive. I have come to realize that for them to live with the guilt of what they did must be so much harder than for me to live with the harm they inflicted on me.

Li Tingting - Tingting is a Chinese campaigner and activist for gender equality and sexuality. Tingting set up a Lesbian Community Training Group, offering counselling services and support for university students and has reportedly been put on the Chinese media blacklist, which means no national media will report on or converse with her. The NGO she worked for was also shut down in an example of the lengths the repressive regime will go to silence her. Tingting has written opinion pieces for international media, including "The Guardian," where she describes her arrest and the situation of women's rights in China. She has also participated in discussion panels and given talks on feminism in China in the U.S. and UK.

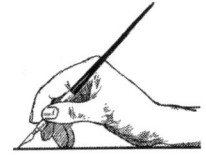

Kim, 55, Indiana, USA

My assault happened when I was 3 years old.

I was living in a foster home when a man in a worker's uniform came into my room. He put a glass in my crib, and asked me if I liked white milk or chocolate milk. I told him chocolate.

He then pulled out his penis and started masterbating into the glass.

I've had many people tell me I couldn't possibly remember what happened to me when I was 3. That's just not true. I remember everything about his pale, ruddy, fat face. I still get shaky and nauseous whenever I see a man who resembles him.

I often wonder where the foster parents were when this happened.

Malala Yousafzai - This courageous young woman rose to fame with her memoir, "I Am Malala," documenting her fearless journey as a young student fighting for access to education in Pakistan. She is an activist and a 2014 Nobel Prize winner. Malala travels the world advocating for education rights for women and children through her foundation, The Malala Fund. She states, "We cannot all succeed when half of us are held back."

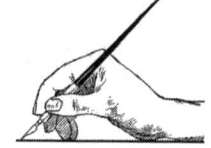

Charity, 27, Arizona, USA

My story is very different than most peoples. As a matter of fact, I have yet to find a story similar to mine, and because of this, I have been told it doesn't count.

I have a very urgent need to tell people that it can happen like this; I need people and my family to understand why I can't just let this go. It has shaped me because I have grown up around it. This is not just my story, but my mom, dad and sister, and my other sister basically counts because she's married to a sexual manipulator.

No one in my family really understands my issue with this. I kind of understand. I feel maybe they have shut down or just can't talk about it, like it's not an issue yet. Also I'm frustrated they can't seem to sympathize with me and that they can defend a pedophile.

First, let me say I was homeschooled right out of kindergarten and I have two older sisters. As a kid, I loved people. I wanted to be friends with everyone and I believed there were no bad people. My oldest sister Sarah felt deprived by being stuck at home all the time. We are pretty sure my dad suffers from PTSD, but we didn't know that at the time. See, my dad gets mad, really mad, and he will throw really big fits. He will yell like a crazy person. We all used to hide while he threw stuff. Basically, it was never a very safe feeling at home. I'm sure Sarah being the oldest had the most trouble with this. She begged to go to public school, and by sixth grade, she got what she wanted.

One day, a boy started following her home. She hated him at first. He wouldn't leave her alone. He said he just wanted to use her phone. It was obvious to me that he was just making excuses. I guess I chose to ignore them because I was too excited to have company. I told myself I was going to keep very close watch. I was playing secret agent. We liked him at first. He was polite and funny and caring. So, even though she hated him, his persistence made her fall in love. She did make him wait a while. I remember when he called at midnight the last day to ask her out. I was 12 when this happened.

Once he became her boyfriend, things blur together. They get kind of nuts; I just wish I had realized it was out of hand sooner. At first, I was glad to have him around. He was comforting and he was the only one who came after me when I cried, no matter how hard I pushed him away. So, when I found out my sister was pregnant at 16, I was happy for her. I was glad to be getting an older brother.

I don't know everything. Even if I could remember everything, it still wouldn't make much sense to me. I do know he told me that if Sarah was not pregnant, then she can't get pregnant at all. He had convinced her to get pregnant on purpose so they could stay together. I wish I had known what manipulation looked like back then.

I remember I used to spend time with them at his mom's house. This is when he started saying stuff. Like saying "It's okay if I try a couple things. Aren't you curious?" I was only 13 when he started working on me. He would say he had already seen me naked and there were cameras in the bathrooms.

I put my defenses up when I knew he wanted me like that. I just thought, if I don't let him, he can't have me or touch me. I have no idea how long he worked on me; I just know he did this while my sister was pregnant. I also know now that she knew the whole time. He even asked for her permission.

Here are my memories:

I remember watching South Park the Movie. I was spending the night at his mom's, staying in the same room as the two of them. While laying down on the floor, I heard my sister crying. He was whispering something to her. She was already six months pregnant. I know now he was asking her if he could get me, and she said yes. Then he came down to the floor and wanted to role play. He took off his pants to get comfortable and asked me to do the same, but I didn't. I can't remember the role playing, I just remember picking the name dick to turn him off.

Next, I remember one time we played truth or dare. I don't remember all of that either, but at the end, he dared me to let him stick his hand down my pants, and I stood there against the wall just waiting for it to stop.

I remember feeling different the next day, or maybe very changed. I still can't find a word for that feeling.

I remember doing everything over time except going "all the way." He kept talking about how I needed to now or he would never get over me. That this will never end. He told me he had seen lots of girls naked and it was no big deal. He used manipulation and pressure to get what he wanted, but never straight up force.

He was there for me a lot. He would come and find me when I cried, which happened often, since people would yell at me. But he would come and sit with me and cheer me up. This became the reason I later would never let anyone see me cry. No matter how desperately I needed it. It is hell to cry for more than three hours and still be too afraid to get help or even tell anyone the next day. Even asking for a hug from someone is still just too hard.

When I finally got three days away from him, I gathered myself up. I knew I couldn't let him have me. I didn't want to. I had to say no. My sister was away at a doctor's appointment with my mom when he came over. My memory skips to the part where we are in my room and I'm on the bed and he's trying to push himself in me. I begged him to stop and told him it hurt. He almost didn't stop, but he did finally let me go. When he left, I cried, but I was still a virgin.

He got my sister involved after that time. She started telling me I needed to "finish or this will never end." I had to shut down my feelings and mind to keep from being controlled by both of them. She even dared me to let him do it once, and that was another close call.

There were a couple times through the years they both tried to get the rest of me. One time when I was 17, he tried to drug me. Once, my sister begged me to give it up so he could get over me and just love her.

I lived like this my entire teenage years, yet still not really understanding what had happened. I heard about stuff like this, but I felt like mine didn't really count, even though it fit the bill. I was always being told that I was being paranoid, and they treated me like I was nuts. My friend and Sarah, my oldest sister, certainly did. Everyone really liked him and they said I should get over it and have some fun.

So, I had to be around him a lot. I got really good at putting my defenses up, to the point even if I was on the verge of a break down, if he came around, I would no longer feel anything.

I had one really good friend. She was loud and protective, and she didn't take anyone's crap. She could see right through him from the start. She kept breaking down my walls to come find me and help me, and having her around kept him away because she was too blunt. He knew better than to try when she was with me. My voice was broken, and she was the only one on my side, or who truly saw me. I believe this girl saved my life. She was able to get through to me, but it would take a long time, and she still hardly ever saw me cry.

Over time I got better. I kept a lot of journals and even wrote a self-help book, which I plan to publish soon.

When I was 18, he told me my sister was pregnant, but there was a chance she may not be able to have this baby. He said he would make her have an abortion if I didn't give it up. I said no and he told me and my whole family I couldn't see her anymore. She did actually get an abortion.

My life kind of got out of hand after that. I was so mad I just started telling everyone the truth. That's when it started, I guess. I no longer believed in this being a secret. I have so much more understanding now and I can talk about it, but talking about how it affected me is still really hard. I became determined to leave, so my mom could see her grandkids again, and because I realized it was only a matter of time before he used force on me to get what he wanted.

I finally left. I moved from Texas to Arizona when I was 21, and I Instantly got better. I have had a few hard times, but I won't ever go back because nothing will ever compare to that.

I am now 27 years old. I have been married for four years to the best guy ever, and I am able to cry on him. I feel safe, and that's more than I could ever ask for. We have two kids, a 3-year-old girl and a 2-year-old boy.

My sister is still with that same man, and he has manipulated her into a lot of bad stuff, but he is currently serving 10 years in jail for downloading child pornography, and I hope it is a wake up call for her.

Marie de Gournay 1565-1645 - a French writer, de Gournay wrote a number of literary compositions, including two proto-feminist works, "The Equality of Men and Women" and "The Ladies' Grievance."

Julie, 17, California, USA

I met the first boy I would ever love when I was in seventh grade.

In eighth grade, I developed a major crush on him (he was crushing on me, too, but I didn't know that until later).

Freshman year of high school, we became best friends. We were absolutely inseparable. When I say he was my other half, I mean it. I had never connected with someone as deeply as with him. We had everything in common and we could talk for hours about anything and everything. Everything felt so easy.

We dated for two years. He is the first and only person I've ever loved. I lost my virginity to him. Throughout the course of our relationship he was emotionally abusive, but never physically harmed me. That is until one day, when I told him I didn't want to have sex. I was on my period and was upset with him because of a fight we'd had earlier. But he was persistent. I repeatedly told him no, but he wouldn't listen. He insisted I was just being a tease. I allowed him to take off my shirt, but I drew the line there. But he wasn't satisfied.

He pinned me down, ripped off my bottoms, and pulled out my tampon. I was humiliated.

The entire time I was telling him to stop, and tried to push him off me, but he was a whopping 5-foot-10 and 150 pounds compared to my 5-foot-0 and 104 pounds. He proceeded to shove his dick inside me and fucked me without letting go of my hands, which were pinned above my head. I tried to squirm away, but then he pinned my arms with one hand and my waist with the other until he came. As soon as he came, he let go and I screamed at him for doing what he did.

I told him he raped me and he was in shock.

He claimed he thought I was joking around and being playful. I will never forget the day I was raped by the boy I thought was my soulmate. I was left with bruising on my waist and around my wrists from where he had me pinned down. I was 16. I gave him everything, but it was never enough for him. I left him soon after this event, but not soon enough.

I am scarred from my experience with him. I loved him in a way I'll never be able to love again and he hurt me more than I'll ever hurt again. I'm terrified of being vulnerable with anyone else and in fear of being hurt, but I know it won't compare to the pain I endured when I realized the one I loved would never truly love me. He told me I was being dramatic.

I told a couple friends about it much later, but they brushed it off and said something about how "that's just how guys are."

Mary Anne Warren – 1946 – 2010 Warren is the author of "Gendercide: The Implications of Sex Selection," a 1985 book exploring the targeting of extermination of women and abuses against them both in history and in current times.

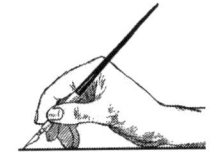

Tamara, 40, California, USA

Raised in a home of sadness and despair, my father died before he could be there; I knew no where to look for someone to care.

The teenage boy next door took my hand, invited me to come and be his friend. A precious moment of admiration and love, I felt like I was invited to join an adventure.

Avoiding his sister, my best friend, we ran off to hatch a secret shenanigan. Something fun, private, shared.

We snuck into the old garage and slid under that old Pinto Wagon up on blocks, and he laid me down on the stained, greasy, old carpet.

"Hush," he said, as he pulled my pants down. I looked away. Out of the corner of my eye seeing my single mother with the lawnmower go by.

Taught to listen to those older than I, I laid still and silently cried.

I know what happened, but can't remember why. And why again, and thrice besides.

In a moment of comfort and care one night, I told my mother what we did out of sight. Expecting reassurance, love and insight, I was in for quite a fright.

Tearfully she ran from me straight for the phone to translate the fate of how to condone, imploding and exploding, enough for the both of us.

Her uncivilized shouts of justice, impaired by nothing of care for me.

The police were quickly called to bear. Terrifying a mind too young to compare right, wrong, trouble, disgrace.

Who did what and where was the mistake?

All I knew was it was all unsafe.

My bedroom, which locked from inside, was my place.

Hours of begging and pleading it took for me to open the door, a chicken pot pie won entry eventually, and a lifetime of comfort food was born.

A lesson unrivaled: I was in the only place which was safe.

I was the master of my own space.

I was 3.

Welcome to your soul, your heart, yourself. The reliable source of love, stability, peace, kindness, discernment, and survival.

It's good to know you're there in a pinch.

Mary Wollstonecraft - Wollstonecraft is the most-cited feminist writer of the late 18th century. She is generally characterized as the first feminist philosopher. Her 1792 book, "A Vindication of the Rights of Woman" is one of the first feminist works. Wollstonecraft believed that both genders contributed to inequality. She espoused that a woman having considerable power over a man was taken for granted, and both genders required education to promote the necessary attitudinal changes.

Ella, 19, Aarhus, Denmark

When I was 18, my girlfriend and I went to this street-food festival in Aarhus. It was in a big open warehouse which had been made into a dining area, filled with food carts from different parts of the world. The place had just opened, so there were a lot of people. It was impossible not to brush up against the other guests at the venue which was a bit uncomfortable, but to be expected. I had lowered my expectations for personal space for the night.

I was standing in line for a Vietnamese cart that seemed popular, discreetly holding hands with my girlfriend, when a large man walked up behind me. Even considering how cramped the place was, he was standing VERY CLOSE. I could feel him brushing up against my ass and my back. I am quite small, so he his presence felt intimidating to me.

During the wait, he brushed against my back with increasing frequency. I wasn't initially conscious of how uncomfortable I felt, after all, it was a tight space, closeness was to be expected. But my girlfriend gave me a concerned look and I realized I was squeezing her hand very hard and inching closer and closer to her, while trying to get away from the man.

I nudged her forward a bit to get some space for myself and her, but the man stepped forward, too, right back in my personal bubble, so his body was partially pressed against mine. He was even closer than before. I could hear him breathing heavily over all the noise in the warehouse. I looked around at the other people in the line and no one else was standing so close. It was weird. I looked up at him, but he was staring directly ahead.

The disconnect between ignoring me with his eyes and intensely focusing on me with his body was EXTREMELY uncomfortable and confusing. He moved closer still.

When I got to where I was supposed to order my food, I could feel the stranger all over my back. I was physically panicked, but at the same time, I couldn't bring myself to make a scene.

I was in a line. People were SUPPOSED to take up as little space as possible. Every time I tried to pull away, which was quite a lot, he would put himself closer to me. I felt like he was somehow angry. This was aggressive behavior. It was only 10 minutes that the stranger had been grinding against me, but the feeling stayed with me the rest of the evening. I felt as if I had done something wrong.

I caught myself hunching my shoulders and making my body smaller all week. I STILL take up as small of a space as possible in most situations involving strangers. It wasn't the only time a stranger has disrespected my personal space or even ground up against me in public, but it was definitely the most prolonged and aggressive instance.

I will never know if the stranger was intentionally touching me or just passive aggressively telling me I was in his way, either way the message was clear: I don't have to respect your personal space.

Mohja Kahf – Born in 1967, Kahf is a Muslim feminist from Damascus, Syria. She is an Arab poet, novelist, and professor at the University of Arkansas. Her works explore themes of cultural dissonance and Arab and Muslim identities and practices in a humorous way. She reconfigures Islamic women in a more progressive image of Islam. She also gives support to her fellow writers of the "twisted revolution," saying, "Poetry is a witness."

Khalid, 30, United Arab Emirates

This is my first time ever sharing my story in full detail. I tried to suppress this memory for so long that I'm actually surprised I still remember it so vividly.

At the time of my childhood, we had a small and close to each other kind of society. Adults were to be trusted and respected. As most people in the community knew each other, there was no concept of "stranger danger." Or at least, it wasn't a big concern.

I was only 10 or 11 years old when I got raped.

I was playing football with the neighborhood kids. I got tired from playing, so I got out and sat by myself nearby to catch my breath.

A man in his mid-30s approached me out of nowhere and said his son accused me of beating him. I didn't know him personally, but I'd seen him around before, so I didn't see him as a threat. Of course, I denied beating his son because no such thing had ever happened. He said he lived nearby and I should go with him so that his son could verify it wasn't me. I was so eager to prove my innocence that I stupidly went with him without doubting anything.

We entered a nearby building and he said the elevator would take a long time and we should take the stairs instead as they lived on the first floor. The stairs in my country are not open for everyone to see. Each floor has a door that leads to the stairs, which makes it isolated from the rest of the building. Again, stupidly I went with him and didn't suspect anything.

As soon as we got into the stairs, he said he didn't want to be unfair to me and his son had told him the person who had beaten him had a birthmark on his back. So the guy told me that I should show him my back so he could make sure it wasn't me. Another obvious lie I fell for.

I turned around and lifted my shirt to show him how I didn't have any birthmarks on my back. At this point, he surrounded me with his arms and rubbed himself on me. I tried to resist, but he was a lot stronger than I was. He then released his arms and tried to pull down my pants. I tried to push him and run away, but he grabbed me by the neck and squeezed hard.

He said, "If you don't resist, it will be quick and painless."

I feared for my life and stopped resisting. I just stood there hoping to God he'd finish quickly, or that I would die, or that anything would happen to make it stop. When he did what he did and finished, he got dressed and told me to stay there for five minutes and then come out. He said, if I didn't do that, he would do it to me again and "this time it will be a lot more painful."

Again, stupidly I followed his orders. I didn't have a watch, so I counted the seconds in my head. I've never been more afraid in my life.

I never saw him again. I think he was lurking around our neighborhood looking for the right opportunity, and he got it.

After the five minutes was over, I ran back home. It took all the strength I had not to cry, so that no one would ask me what was wrong. I got home and locked myself in the bathroom for a long time, crying and trying to clean myself.

Then came the flood of questions. Why would a man want to have sex with me, a boy? What did I do to deserve this?

Then I started to blame myself. I must have done something to encourage him. I was too stupid to see the obvious signs and stop it from ever happening. Because I haven't told anyone, he's still walking around probably doing the same thing to other boys. Everyone he raped after that day is because of me.

I felt like a girl, that I'm of sexual interest for men. I was emasculated before even becoming a man. I stopped wearing shorts or short sleeves. I didn't show any skin and hid in baggy clothing. On top of all that, I had to go on like nothing had happened. I had to go to school daily and face the scary adults. Whenever I passed by two or more men, I trembled in fear. I felt like dying everyday. I stopped trusting anyone, and I still don't.

The only reason that I sort of moved on is because, as I grew into an adult male, the probability of it ever happening again diminished. I feel so bad for the ladies who don't have such luxury.

Now, 20 years later, I'm still not 100 percent over it. I have serious trust issues. I still get nervous in predominantly male places. I'm still uncomfortable showing my skin, especially in places like gyms and locker rooms. I try to go there at weird times so I'm either alone, or there are very few people.

Still, after all these years, I am ashamed of it. Ashamed of how stupid and naïve I was, ashamed I still feel like a "lesser" man, ashamed others might been hurt because I didn't report him.

Rosie The Riveter - Although her character may be fictional, Rosie the Riveter encompassed the female strength championed throughout the feminist movement. Representing the women who worked throughout World War II, the empowering female symbol remains an icon to this day, reminding us of the incredible female efforts during the 1940s.

Lisa, 44, New Jersey, USA
WHY NOW?

So, I have sat back and watched all of the news reports and read the articles and statements of so many victims. I haven't commented much or spoken out. Definitely I have not spoken out.

Now I feel the need to.

I am seeing comments like "Why didn't they report it?" and "Why didn't she say something sooner?" "Why now? Why is so much coming out now? Why are so many women all of a sudden talking about what happened to them?"

Well, let me explain something to you -- especially those of you who have been extremely lucky enough to not have gone through anything like those people. You will never, ever, know the amount of shame a sexual assault victim experiences. It doesn't matter the age -- a child, a teenager, an adult. You are left feeling disgusted, afraid, embarrassed, alone, and ashamed.

The first time someone touches you, especially as a child, you have no idea what to do. No matter how much you have been taught to scream and run away, tell someone, whatever. You freeze. You are in shock. Afraid to move.

If you are lucky, you can actually get your brain to form the words and get yourself to say "NO!" or "Stop!" But sometimes you are too afraid to speak or even breathe. You are stuck. Frozen. Shaking. Crying -- silently. You try to push them away, but it doesn't matter. They just keep going. Then you just want it to be over. You feel like you are outside of your body watching what is happening. You focus on anything else to distract you from thinking about what is happening. The door. The wall. The clock.

The TV. The TV ... '"Happy Days" is playing ... how ironic.
Sometimes it's a single incident, other times it happens over and over for years. It's strangers, friends, family members, significant others. Sometimes it is the one you trust most. Then the perpetrator will tell you it's all YOUR fault, or that you will get in trouble if you tell anyone, or they threaten you with harm. Sometimes they NEVER SAY A WORD.

No incident is "not as bad" as someone else's. There isn't a scale of 1-10. Ask any victim; it's all a 10. They were violated -- every ounce of their being was assaulted. Their body, their mind, their sense of safety and trust, and their soul. They are affected for the rest of their lives. They have to carry this burden forever.

Oh, and you want to talk about telling someone? You don't even have to be threatened to "Keep your mouth shut!" It doesn't matter. Remember, you don't want anyone to know. YOU don't even want to know. It's finally over. You just want to forget it happened. Yet it consumes you and you can't forget it. No matter how hard you try. And you will never forget. It becomes burned into your existence.

You cope any way you can -- becoming numb, depressed, withdrawn, turning to alcohol, drugs, falling into self-harm, suffering a mental breakdown. Over time, you will be triggered -- by something on TV, something someone does or says to you, a scent, or seeing the perpetrator. You will panic and feel like you are experiencing it all over again.

Sometimes you are forced to continue to have that person in your life. You have no control. So you try to avoid him as much as possible. You come up with every excuse to never be around him. "It seems like you are always sick on the holidays!" Yep. Every excuse, it only helps a little. Sitting upstairs in your bedroom, crying and cutting, while the rest of your family celebrates the holidays and has an amazing time downstairs without you. But it's okay. This is what is best. This is what is safest. This is what you need.

This is why...

Ava, 32, California, USA
Me Too

I recall when the news broke about Harvey Weinstein and his decades of sexual assault and harassment toward women. It was shocking to me only because I wondered how it had remained unknown to the world for so long. With a clear pattern of abuse happening, how could it not have come to light long before? Then I recalled my own story.

Predators prey on you with threats, fear, and bribery to ensure their victim's silence. Harvey Weinstein used money and threats of blackballing careers to silence his victims. My abuser used the threat of harming my loved ones to keep me silent.

I was 4 years old the first time it happened. It was my father. That kind of betrayal by someone whom you're supposed to trust more than anyone in the whole world is hard to put into words.

It hurts because you wonder why you couldn't have had the loving father you see other kids having. My abuse continued for four years and only ended when I was given a physical by a doctor who discovered that I had a broken hymen at only 8 years old.

What followed was typical of what we have seen in this #metoo campaign: blaming the victim. My mother didn't press charges because I begged her not to. I didn't think that I had the courage it would take to put myself through that. Having to relive it over and over so publicly would have possibly broken me for life.

There are days I regret that decision. I would have liked to have seen him get what he deserved. But most days I know that at that age I was broken down and I didn't have the strength it would have taken to fight back.

So instead, my mother decided to simply pursue full custody. It wasn't easy at that point in the '90s. Courts weren't as readily on the mother's side, and my father and his attorney fought back by saying my mother was making me say these horrible things just so she could have custody of me and my brother.

It goes to show how broken my mind was because I started to wonder if that was the truth. Maybe I had made the whole thing up. I held on to that thought in the back of my head for a long time because I wanted it to be true. I so wanted it to be true because then I wouldn't feel the way I did. I felt like nothing. Like I didn't matter. It was what my abuser had reduced me to.

The custody case was harrowing for me. I couldn't eat or sleep. I eventually made myself so sick from fear and worry my mother had to take me to the hospital in the middle of the night. I recall that trip. I was so afraid he would just appear out of the shadows. While the court case was going on, I stayed with my mother and my grandmother, but I knew there was a real possibility my father could come and take me away.

It was so hard to live with the thought of it that my body turned against me. We made it to the hospital and the doctor told my mother what I already knew: There was nothing physically wrong with me. It was psychological and I should see a therapist.

I remember leaving the following morning, and as my mother and the doctor spoke further inside the entrance, I saw my father leaning against the wall in the courtyard. He simply looked at me. It shook me to my core. I didn't know how much more I could take. Fortunately, my mother soon won custody and we moved away for a fresh start.

I've attempted therapy a few times over the years, but I've never stuck to it. It always leaves me feeling emotionally spent. Having to revisit those memories and speak about them is so taxing for me. I also feel a shrink with no similar experience couldn't adequately help me in getting past my issues. Most likely I am wrong about that, and I hope I find the courage one day to finally get some real help.

It has been more than two decades since I left my childhood home, but I know I am still stuck in the past, because there are residual things which make up who I am which are a direct result of my abuse. I have an extreme fear about trusting men. I don't have regular relationships with men at all

Commitment isn't something I can do. I have also put on weight as a way of insulating myself from appearing attractive to men. I don't wish to get married or ever have children. To say my childhood has impacted my adult life is putting it mildly.

I avoid a lot of things in life and convince myself the small world I have made for myself is enough. It's safe and that is what I so desperately need. I don't ever want to feel the fear I did as a child. As a teen and woman, there have been times I have been a victim of sexual harassment and inappropriate behavior from men, and it always leaves me retreating into myself and feeling anxious about being victimized all over again.

Clearly, this is no way to live, but I also don't know how else to go about it. Even if therapy allows me to better deal with life, there will always be predatory men out there. I will always be trying to protect myself from harm at the hands of a man and that just doesn't allow for total trust in the opposite sex. So I am right back at square one. I am envious of sexual assault survivors who seem to have forged a life for themselves without the past rearing its ugly head in their daily lives. I wonder how they have the strength to do it. How do you look at the world and not be afraid of the "monster" around every corner?

It is no way to live and it is why I hope the conversations we are being forced to have today will bring changes to how men interact with women on a daily basis. Truth be told, predators will always be predators. They cannot change, but the laws can. Women are in need of more strenuous laws that protect us.

After all this time, having to still tweet #stopviolenceagainstwomen is exhausting. I don't want this to be such a doom and gloom post. I have come a very long way. I am no longer suicidal, I no longer take medication for anxiety and depression, and I finally attend college after being afraid for years to be out in the world where I could be in unsafe situations. I take part in life around me now more than I ever have.

I have a long way to go, but I have come so far. I just remind myself to take it one day at a time. That is how I am going to make it through this. My father doesn't get to take my future the way he took my childhood.

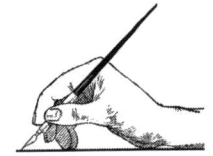

Jenn, 21, Maryland, USA

My name is Jenn, I am 21 years old, and I am a sexual abuse survivor.

I was adopted from Kiev, Ukraine, when I was 6 months old. As a little girl, all I wanted was to be "daddy's little girl," but he was just always more interested in the things my brother was doing.

Shortly after I turned 9, my father started molesting me. He also started sleeping in the basement instead of with my mother so she wouldn't notice him getting up in the middle of the night.

I was 11 the first time he raped me. I also started developing, physically, rather quickly at this time. I started starving myself because I thought maybe if I didn't have boobs, he would stop. He didn't.

For my 13th birthday, the only present I asked for was a lock on my bedroom door. Although I got the lock on my door, it didn't last long since my mother soon broke it while kicking the door.

When I was 13, I became pregnant, and as soon as my father found out, he took me to get an abortion. There were absolutely no questions asked when I went to get the procedure. I guess money really can make anything go away. After that, he got smarter and started using a condom.

At 15, he began to bring his "friends" over, one of whom was my uncle. I didn't think there was a level of pain greater than the one I felt at 11 years old, but there was. I went to the hospital one morning after he had brought four friends in the night before and I wouldn't stop bleeding. I ended up getting internal and external stitches. Again, no questions asked. Everything just went back to my "normal."

Throughout all of this, various teachers and soccer coaches of mine had reported suspicious bruises and marks they saw.

Unfortunately the compassion, empathy, and nurturing you see on "SVU" isn't always what you are met with from law enforcement. I did, however, have TV Olivia Benson, and real life Mariska Hargitay too, in a way, fill the role of a protective, nurturing, compassionate, mother figure I never had. I am working on moving out of my parents' home now, which will hopefully happen soon so I never have to see them again. My mother has known about it since I was 10 and has never stopped it.

Since I unfortunately do not yet have a close to this chapter in my life, I'll end this with saying: 11 years, multiple suicide attempts, and countless sleepless nights later, I am currently studying to become a child and adolescent psychologist specializing in trauma. I will help children who cannot help themselves.

Something good has to come from this, right?

Ruth Bader Ginsberg - Before her tenure as a Supreme Court justice, Bader Ginsburg co-founded the "Women's Rights Law Reporter" in 1970, the first U.S. law journal to focus exclusively on women's rights. Two years later, she co-founded the Women's Rights Project at the American Civil Liberties Union (ACLU), once again making sure women's voices were heard in law. Appointed by President Bill Clinton in 1993, Bader Ginsburg became the second female Supreme Court justice ever, a position she still holds today and she uses it to advocate for women's rights.

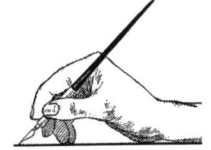

Mel, 15, Ohio, USA

At a young age, I had grown up close to relatives and family, unaware of the adult problems and family feuds spewing about. All I cared for were those days when my relatives and family all came together in unison for a joyous holiday. Or even for just a normal, laid back day. My Nan and Pap's House was "party central," and still is to this day. Birthdays, reunions. Their house was the prime destination at which my family and I, and all the relatives would meet together for a day without stress or work.

I was just 5 or 6 years old. Smiling confidently and never being pried away from the arms of a loved one. I had grown so close to all those I knew, for the world at that age to me was only my small hometown.

Trust was something I gave fully to those around me. Especially my own abuser, who shall remain nameless.

I don't remember how it started; I only remember the glimpses of how I was touched in the basement of my Nan and Pap's house. Every time I would go, full of laughter and excitement for time well-spent with family, I had really only focused on one person. My idol and my everything, a male cousin of mine.

I loved the games he played, watching him shoot a variety of not only animated humans, but also a drastic number of tentacled aliens and creatures alike. But little had I known, the game he played with me was much worse than blood and shootings on a TV screen.

His hands ran along my body and I was eager to obey his every word, for I thought there was no one else who I trusted and loved more than the man I looked up to, my own blood relative. I remember the countless whispers that ran through his lips as he felt me, and I had stayed silent.

"This is between us, okay?"

"After, I'll let you play the game with me."

I nodded eagerly, wanting nothing but affection due to the lack of friendship I had at that young age.

One day, it changed. I smiled and giggled happily, talking with my mother of games and activities cousins do together. I told her without blinking, twinkles in my eye, thinking maybe she had played the same games as me. Because, of course, I knew nothing of sexual abuse or molestation at such a young age. Yet I had been abused.

My mother quickly called my male cousin's mother; they talked for quite a while. I only remember that I was apparently called a "liar" by his mother. But, of course, who could accept or would want to accept the fact their child had sexually assaulted someone else's child?

Of course, she bluntly asked my cousin, her son, if he had done what I had claimed. He said no, denying and getting away with what he had done.

No reports, restraining orders, or anything of the like were made; a simple phone call, no punishment, and that was that.

I am now 15. I have my driving permit, have lost weight, and am at a healthy mental and physical state.

But, to this day, I face my abuser unresolved. I face him at the same place where the assaults happened. I see him ignore me, I see how his girlfriend is happy and giggly around him as if he were the best man in the world. His family is proud of whom he has become, for they are unaware of his doings to me. No one has spoken of my abuse. Most of them don't even know of my abuse, and if they were to, they would most likely not believe me.

But I know what happened. I remember few details, but can feel his hands touch me to this day and remember how he used me like a rag doll.

If someone I know is reading this, please understand that I do not dislike my family. I am only uncomfortable with the thought my abuser is still in the same building and environment as I am. I do not blame them, but blame those who knew and continued to keep quiet.

If you have known someone abused: Please do something about it, for if she or he must continue to face the abuser even though the abuse may have ended, the abuse may very well start up again. And the one who has been abused will never acquire the healing that is truly needed and deserved.

I am Mel. And thank you for reading my story.

Sheryl Sandberg - The Facebook COO is responsible for pioneering the "Lean In" movement with her 2013 book of the same name encouraging women to excel in the workforce. Through her prominent position at Facebook, her work with the Lean In Foundation and the Women for Women International Board, Sandberg is outspoken about the inequality women face in the workforce. Recently, she teamed up with Gloria Steinem to empower young girls following the 2016 presidential election. "We need women at all levels, including the top, to change the dynamic, reshape the conversation, to make sure women's voices are heard and heeded, not overlooked and ignored."

Luna, 16, Netherlands

13 years old.

I didn't really want to meet up, but I said yes.
I told him I didn't want to kiss or do anything sexual.
But that day ended up being my head's biggest mess.

I remember the disgust while I went home on my bike.
I remember every word he said and every look he gave me.
But what I remember the most is how we got into a fight.

He tried so hard to open my jeans; I fought so hard to keep myself clean.
Clean from him and clean from shame.
Clean, so clean so that when leaving I would still be the same.

I didn't realize until 3 years later.
Me and my 13-year-old body were touched by a stranger.
Someone who shouldn't have. Someone who I now can call a raper.

I knew the boy. I call him a stranger because he was never a friend. He was younger than me, I think.

I never reported him because I didn't realize it until last year. I always had this feeling of being uncomfortable when thinking about subjects like rape and I didn't understand where it came from.

One time, I was showering and it just dropped like on a bomb on me. I started to write down everything that happened that day and I was never so ashamed of myself. It's too late now to report him. But I really wanted to share my story and have it said. I never told anyone. I always just say the boy I lost my virginity to was not a nice person.

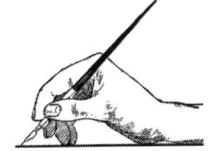

Emily, 20, Vermont, USA

I went out to the bars with my friends one night, but that's about all I remember. I recall arriving at the bar, but I don't remember drinking, talking to anyone, etc. I woke up in a daze, completely naked in a bed in a room I did not recognize.

I turned to see him. I had met him at a party once, we followed each other on social media, but he was two years older and I had never thought to be intimately involved with him. I had absolutely zero recollection of seeing him, or leaving the bar with him that previous night.

If I had been conscious of the situation, I would not have left with him. Quickly grabbing my clothes, which were thrown across the room, I left, walking past an empty condom wrapper on my way out. That's the only way I knew we had sex.

Had I given verbal consent? Did he ask me if I was comfortable doing anything? Did I say YES? Very unlikely. I will never know. What I do know is he took a very drunk girl home with him and completely took advantage of her.

I still feel violated to this day, months later. I've only told my boyfriend and best friend.

Simone de Beauvoir - An outspoken political activist, writer, and social theorist, in 1949 de Beauvoir wrote "The Second Sex," an ahead-of-its-time book credited with paving the way for modern feminism. In this influential and extremely controversial book, de Beauvoir critiques the patriarchy and social constructs faced by women. "The point is not for women simply to take power out of men's hands, since that wouldn't change anything about the world. It's a question precisely of destroying that notion of power."

Matthew L., 33, Texas, USA

"*Show me your war face!*" *is a term used in United States Marine Corps training, meant to intimidate the enemy. I started MyWarFace.org to encourage other victims to come forward with their heads held high. There is nothing to be ashamed of and, most importantly, it is never the victim's fault. The perpetrators are cowards and prey on the weak and vulnerable. It is time to show our faces. To stop hiding and demand justice for the things that happened to us. If I had the courage to speak up many years ago, my rapist would have been in jail. But now he walks the street as a free man. Speak up now.*

"I was a bully," CK said. This was during a recorded phone conversation I was having with my childhood rapist while working with police and the district attorney's office of Westchester County, New York, in late 2017.

CK did have similar characteristics to a bully. He was significantly bigger, taller, and stronger than I was, and five years my senior. Most 4-year-olds are rather helpless against a 9-year-old, as are most 9-year-olds against a 14-year-old.

CK often hurt me physically, belittled me, and made threats against my life, but the difference between a stereotypical neighborhood bully and CK is the constant rape which I and other children had to endure for nearly a decade.

Playdates, weekends, birthday parties and holidays, which I've been told are cherished moments for many children, are dark and partially repressed memories for me of being threatened and viciously raped. After years of sexual assault, his flaccidity turned into erections and his threats became deeper and darker.

Aside from what I could refer to as "normal" sexual acts between two consenting adults, CK had myself and other children perform strange and unusual acts. Whether it was "stretching exercises" when he would take turns pulling out our genitals as far as they could reach, standing in line swinging our genitals as he masturbated, increasing our tolerance for testicular torture, playing video games as I performed oral sex on him, or forcing me to preform cunnalingus on a young girl as she attempted to scream for help. Her screams were met by CKs hands, dragging her by the hair and down an entire flight of steps as she attempted to escape. He was clearly dangerous and capable of severe physical harm. CK would always tell us if we told an adult, he would kill us.

I believed him.

I remember one specific time, CK sat us down in front of a drawing he had done of an underground dungeon with many different rooms and compartments all designed for his sexual fantasies. We were told we'd start construction in the following days -- forced labor. And like slaves, we were forced to dig at his parents' property. Needless to say, a small group of children with shovels were not able to complete his sex dungeon, and we were sexually assaulted again for our poor efforts.

Not only did my parents know, they didn't stop it. Many adults knew and did nothing.

I contacted CK's father, also on a recorded line. He admitted to knowing about what CK had done to me, saying " ... you are not telling me anything I didn't already know about."

After keeping my secret for decades, and armed with these and other recorded conversations, I finally believed this sick and twisted individual would be brought to justice. But I found out the district attorney could not press charges against CK because of an antiquated statute of limitations. I suppose the good news is the law was changed around 2005, however, it is not retroactive.

The last correspondence I had from law enforcement was on November 8, 2017, at 8:52 a.m. Central Time, from a detective at the Westchester County special victims unit:

Matthew,

I am sorry, but I have been advised that we will not be conducting any further investigations due to the time that has passed and no incidents or victims that have come forward that are within the time limits of the law. Detective [name redacted]

On CK's own public social media pages he has posted "throwback pictures" from the 1980s, with references to him playing the same entertainment systems he had when he raped me and others. There are pictures of him holding a small child and one of his victims commented on it.

According to Linkedin, CK works in the music industry. According to his website biography, CK has worked in Hollywood on scores for famous movies, as well as television scores for well-known shows.

I find it rather ironic that in 2009, I was serving my country in Afghanistan as a corporal in the United States Marine Corps, which had its own low points in life for me, meanwhile my rapist was laughing it up and taking private pictures in the White House.

This ends now. I've shown my war face, it's time we collectively show the world ours.

Sojourner Truth - Born Isabella Baumfree, 1797 – 1883. Truth was an African-American abolitionist and women's rights activist. She was born into slavery in Ulster County, New York, and escaped to freedom with her infant daughter in 1826. After going to court to recover her son, she became the first black woman to win such a case against a white man in 1828. During the Civil War, Truth helped recruit black troops for the Union Army. In 2014, Truth was included in Smithsonian magazine's list of the "100 Most Significant Americans of All Time." One memorable quote from Truth is, "If the first woman God ever made was strong enough to turn the world upside down all alone, these women together ought to be able to turn it back, and get it right side up again! And now they is asking to do it, the men better let them."

Misty Griffin, 35, California, USA

Editor's Note: Misty Griffin is the best-selling author of "Tears of the Silenced," her memoir of abuse, leaving the Amish community, and speaking out about her experiences. Her book has already sold more than 100,000 copies and she is active in speaking out and raising awareness for sexual abuse in religious communities. This is part of her story.

I think all survivors of sexual abuse deal with hesitancy when telling their story. I did. I kept my tragic life story to myself and tried to appear normal on the outside, and I was pretty successful at it.

Eight years after leaving the Amish, I finally sat down and started typing my memoir, Tears of the Silenced. I had spent those previous eight years trying to forget my terrible childhood and the horrifying assault that had been the reason for my leaving the Amish church.

I was held in captivity until I was nearly 19, and then at age 23, I was sexually assaulted and threatened by the bishop of my Amish church.

All of those years after leaving the Amish, I hid the pain and the nightmares, and only a couple people knew my story. Then, in July of 2013, I realized the only way to keep someone else from going through what I did was to write about it. As I began to type, I truly never imagined that my story would resonate with so many people.

Telling our stories is such a powerful way of raising awareness and encouraging others who have gone through similar situations. Realizing they are not alone is one of the most uplifting things a survivor can experience; there are others out there who understand your pain, and who believe you. This compilation of stories is meant for just that reason, to raise awareness and let survivors out there know: **you are not alone.**

My Life and My Story

I was not born Amish. I was born into a family full of poverty, domestic violence, and drug and alcohol abuse. When I was 4, my mom met a new guy who soon became my stepfather, and that was the beginning of a terrifying nightmare which would last 19 years.

Gradually, we began to dress and live like the Amish. My stepfather eventually cut off almost all access to the outside world. My sister and I were held on a mountain ranch that was six miles from the nearest town. It was a terrifying life full of severe beatings, sexual abuse, and isolation. Being so completely isolated from the rest of the world was probably one of the worst things I went through.

At the age of 18, I finally attempted to escape, after my stepfather tried to break my neck. I was not successful. Fearing my sister and I would eventually escape, my mom and stepdad took my sister and me to an Amish community, where we were adopted and became baptized members.

For three and a half years, I lived as a young Amish woman, but I found that life to be frustrating, and I was concerned by the amount of abuse I was told about and even witnessed.

During my last six months among the Amish, I lived with the bishop's family. Right from the start, the bishop began fondling me and exposing himself to me. I gritted my teeth and bore the abuse; I knew if I told I would be blamed for attracting him.

During the last few months, I began to suspect that he was also molesting his daughters. Then one morning, he came into my room while I was still in bed and assaulted me.

Afterward, I ran to a neighbor lady and she took me to the police. It was a horrifying experience, and in the end the bishop escaped into Canada with his whole family. Eleven years later, I would find out he had molested almost all of his 11 children. While he had been in our community, the church knew he was a child molester and did nothing to stop him.

I believe my real healing began when I decided to write my memoir. With every page I wrote I felt the healing taking place. For the first time in my life, I was actually, truly realizing how much I had been through and how I had tried to save others. Even if I failed, at least I tried.

A year after my book was published, I was contacted by the bishop's oldest daughter and was overjoyed to find out they had come back from Canada and her father was now in police custody.

The detective on the case read my memoir and had figured out the man he was investigating was the bishop in the book. The children recognized me immediately from the book and contacted me through Goodreads. The bishop is now in prison and the children have started their own journey of healing. We keep in contact and I am like a big sister to them.

After my own long journey, a difference had been made. It did not happen right away, but it did eventually.

Survivors of abuse should never stop telling their stories. Our stories might be able to save someone else, as abusers rarely have only one victim. I hope you find encouragement in the following pages and realize the depth of courage of the survivors who have shared their stories.

May our voices never be silenced. With our stories of survival, we can make the world a better a place.

Susan Brownell Anthony - Anthony was an American social reformer and women's rights activist during the women's suffrage movement. Elizabeth Cudy Stanton became her lifelong friend in 1851, and together they founded the Women's Loyal National League in 1863, leading to the largest petition drive in U.S. history at the time. They collected signatures in support of the abolition of slavery and in 1866 initiated the American Equal Rights Association, campaigning for equal rights of women and African Americans. Stanton and Anthony also created a women's rights newspaper called "The Revolution" and began the National Woman Suffrage Association, which eventually merged with the American Woman Suffrage Association. She spent her life in support of women's suffrage and equality, giving speeches and proclaiming, "No man is good enough to govern any woman without her consent."

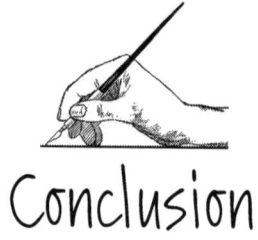

Conclusion

Many of the contributors in this book have found some healing and catharsis in writing their stories out -- some for the first time ever.

While some of these have been incredibly graphic, the nature of sexual assault, abuse, and harassment is not one of ease or simplicity. These are graphic crimes, many of which are never prosecuted.

This book has been incredible to be a part of. To get to know many of these women and men and put them in a position to tell their stories has been gratifying, horrifying, and satisfying.

This book is for them. Each of them came forward and offered their words to me free of any expectations. They simply wanted to speak their truth and I am fortunate enough to have been a part of this truth-telling.

Statistics regarding sexual assault, abuse, and harassment:

• Every 98 seconds someone in the U.S. is sexually assaulted. That means every single day more than 570 people experience sexual violence in the United States.
• Since 1998, it is estimated 17,700,000 women have been victims of rape.
• 99 percent of perpetrators of sexual violence walk free.
• 13 percent of female rape survivors have attempted suicide.
• 64 percent of trans people will experience sexual assault in their lives.
• Trans people of color are 1.8 times more likely to experience sexual violence than Caucasian trans people.
• People ages 16 to 19 are four times more likely than the general population to be victims of rape, attempted rape, or sexual assault.
• Female college students are three times more likely than women in the general population to experience sexual violence. 42 percent of female college rape victims will not report the assault.
• Three percent of men are raped.
• It is estimated 80,600 inmates are victims of rape and assault every year, 60 percent of which is perpetrated by jail or prison staff. ALL sexual contact between inmates and guards is illegal and considered non-consensual.
• A person with a disability is twice as likely to be a victim of sexual violence as those without disabilities.
• An estimated 18,900 military service people experience sexual violence or unwanted sexual contact. One in seven of these victims experienced assault by someone within their chain of command.
• Child protective service agencies estimate approximately 63,000 children are victims of sexual abuse each year.
• 82 percent of all juvenile victims are female and more than 90 percent of adult victims are female.
• Native Americans are twice as likely to experience a rape or sexual assault compared to all other races.

- Only two percent of all sexual assault accusations reported to the police turn out to be false, which is the same rate of false reporting as other types of violent crimes.
- Sexual assault is the violent crime which is least often reported to law enforcement officials. A 2000 study from the Bureau of Justice Statistics of the U.S. Department of Justice found that only 28 percent of victims report their sexual assault to the police.
- One in three women ages 18 to 34 have been sexually harassed and 71 percent say they did not report it.
- In eight out of 10 rape cases, the victim knows the perpetrator.
- 94 percent of women report experiencing PTSD in the first weeks after being raped.
- 40 percent of rape survivors develop STDs as a result of the assault and 80 percent suffer from chronic physical or psychological conditions.

Resources

If you or a loved one has been the victim of sexual assault, abuse, or harassment, please know you are not alone.

You do not have to deal with it or try to heal alone, either.

Here are some resources which can help. If you are able to donate to them, know that you are helping others end the cycle and heal.

RAINN is the Rape, Abuse, & Incest National Network, and is the largest anti-sexual violence organization in the United States. It runs the National Sexual Assault Hotline, which is available 24/7. The number for the hotline is: 800-656-4673.

Girls for Gender Equity is a Brooklyn-based, intergenerational non-profit organization dedicated to strengthening local communities by creating opportunities for young women and girls to live self-determined lives after the trauma of sexual violence. They also help young women tackle the many obstacles young women and girls face such as sexism, racial inequality, homophobia, transphobia, and sexual harassment. Tarana Burke, founder of the Me Too movement, is a Senior Director in this organization and speaks around the world helping women and promoting community healing.

NOW is the National Organization for Women, dedicated to women's rights, and is the largest organization of feminist grassroots activists in the United States. Founded in 1966, NOW's purpose is to promote feminist ideals, lead societal change, eliminate discrimination, and achieve and protect equal rights of all women and girls.

Darkness to Light is a nonprofit organization committed to empowering adults to prevent child sexual abuse. Their crisis hotline is for anyone in the U.S. who needs local information or resources for sexual assault. It is free for both calling 866-FOR-LIGHT (866-367-5444) and texting "Light" to 741741

The Covenant House is a nonprofit dedicated to helping homeless children and stopping human trafficking. Its "nineline" hotline helps people find shelter facilities all across the U.S., Canada, and Central America. The hotline is 800-999-9999.

Male Survivor is an organization dedicated to helping male survivors of sexual assault and abuse. It provides facts, resources, assistance, and support for survivors.

The National Suicide Prevention lifeline is a 24/7 confidential suicide prevention hotline available to anyone in emotional distress or suicidal crisis. You are not alone and the lifeline can help you with professional assistance. The lifeline number is 800-273-8255.

The National Sexual Violence Resource Center is a nonprofit which provides resources for different categories of victims and believes in the power of information, tools, and people.

SATI is Sexual Assault Training & Investigations, is an organization which provides victim-centered multidisciplinary training and expert consultations regarding crimes of sexual assault.

There are also many international resources available to women, men, and children around the world.

Ibiblio.org is one or the largest free information databases online, and has gathered a page with International Rape Crisis Hotlines here.

Together We Are Strong is a Tumblr community, having a safe place for people battling mental illnesses and other struggles. It has compiled a list of international helplines for many countries throughout the world, found here.

Andrew Vachss is an attorney who represents children and youth exclusively, with 30 years of experience in child protective work. He has been a federal investigator in sexually transmitted diseases, a social services caseworker, and a labor organizer. He has put together a list of international helplines for people around the world. List found here: http://www.vachss.com/help_text/index.html

Bios

Author Bio

Jyssica Schwartz is a thirty-something writer, editor, and book coach living in Brooklyn, New York with her husband and a very fluffy cat. She has 10 years of corporate sales and business development experience before she quit her job in early 2017 to pursue being a full-time writer. Building and refining her business has been a challenge and a joy.

Jyssica is often found curled up with a cat and a book, posting pictures of food and cats on Instagram, pithy notes on Twitter, or discussing random thoughts on her Medium blog when she probably should be working.

She holds a Bachelor's degree from the University of Florida and has always been a writer, even before she was getting paid. Jyssica loves music, traveling, rollercoasters, the Yankees, and the Offspring.

Check out her website at www.jyssicaschwartz.com and join her mailing list for rare notes on writer-y things.

About the Designer

Angela Buer is an art educator, specializing in the post-secondary instruction of digital media, fine arts, art history, and humanities. She has been teaching in these disciplines since 2003. She holds an A.A. in Arts, a BFA in Painting and a BA in Art History, as well as a Master's degree in Art Education.

She is an adjunct faculty member at a community college, teaching both online and in the classroom. She teaches courses in graphic design, art, art history, critical thinking, professional development, and the humanities (film, music, art, mythology).

She is a professional art director, production artist, and graphic design

specialist in the coordination of print, web, and other alternative media markets through her company,
Endless Creative World, Inc., www.endlesscreativeworld.com.

If that wasn't enough, she is also the GM for her sister's company, Art of Nursing Care, Inc./Art of Birthing Center in Marina del Rey, CA www.artofnursing.net, and manages - virtually - the day-to-day operations of a midwifery, birth center, and family-wellness practice.

Angela is an artist, feminist, activist, Denver Broncos fan, and a mother of Bengal cats.

Media Inquiries

All press and related inquiries can be directed to:
Josh Lamont, Josh@JRLstrategies.com.

For 20 years, Josh has been working with organizations to advance their missions and realize a better world. He was recently recognized by USA Today and the Wall Street Journal for his work. He is also one of the 8 men who contributed their stories to this book.

In 2010, President Obama appointed Josh as a spokesperson for his administration and as a White House Advance Associate for Michelle Obama and Dr. Jill Biden. He previously held leadership roles at GLSEN, amfAR and was Director of Corporate Giving at Lehman Brothers, where he co-authored Business of Change, highlighting the power of public-private partnerships to change the world.

Josh is now the founder and Chief Mission Accomplice at JRL Strategies (www.JRLstrategies.com), helping organizations and social entrepreneurs advance their missions. A graduate of Cornell, Josh has spent most his career in New York City, Washington, DC, San Francisco, as well as in airports and on sofas around the world.

Historical Feminist Figures

Adam Jones	7
Alice Stone Blackwell	9
Alison Bechdel	13
Alyssa Milano	14
Angela Davis	26
Anita Hill	28
Anna North	33
Anne Dudley Bradstreet	34
Artemisia Gentileschi	40
Asia Argento	41
Barbara Walters	43
Bell Hooks	45
Betty Friedan	52
Brigitte Macron	54
Cecile Richards	61
Chimamanda Ngozi Adichie	62
Cindy Sherman	66
Coretta Scott King	75
Eleanor Roosevelt	77
Elizabeth Cady Stanton	80
Emmeline Pankhurst	88
Frederick Douglass	95
Frida Kahlo	104
Gloria Steinem	109
Hannah Wilke	115
Helen Reddy	117
Hillary Clinton	122
John Stoltenberg	121
John Stuart Mill and Harriet Taylor Mill	128

Katharine Graham	135
Li Tingting	140
Malala Yousafzai	141
Marie de Gournay	146
Mary Anne Warren	148
Mary Wollstonecraft	150
Mohja Kahf	152
Rosie the Riveter	155
Ruth Bader Ginsberg	162
Sheryl Sandberg	165
Simone de Beauvoir	167
Sojourner Truth	170
Susan B Anthony	173

Honorable Mention: The Suffragettes - In both Britain and America, the Suffragettes fought vehemently for women's rights. They were the first major rallying cry for feminism, specifically demanding the the right to vote. Their movements and protests, both peaceful and radical, allowed for the nationwide right for women to vote in America in 1920 and for some women in the United Kingdom the right to vote in 1918, though under 30-year-old non-houseowning women in the U.K. did not get the right to vote until 1928.

A procession of Suffragettes, dressed in white and bearing wreaths and a banner reading "Fight on and God will give the victory" during the funeral proccesion of Emily Davison in Morpeth, Northumberland, 13 June 1913. Crowds line the street to watch.

Six suffragists at the 1920 Republican National Convention in Chicago are seen holding a banner that reads: "No self respecting woman should wish or work for the success of a party that ignores her self. Susan B. Anthony, 1872."

Photo Credits: Photos obtained under U.S. fair use laws and modified so as not to duplicate the integrity or intellectual property thereof. Photo credits are provided when required.

By United States Department of State - Official Photo at Department of State page, Public Domain, https://commons.wikimedia.org/w/index.php?curid=7526134

Sources

Barley, Bethany and Images: Features, Rex. (2017). The Top 50 Most Empowering Feminist Quotes of All Time. *Stylist UK, Life Section*. Cambridgeshire, UK. Retrieved from https://www.stylist.co.uk/life/the-top-50-most-empowering-feminist-quotes-of-all-time-women-suffragette-feminism-angelina-jolie-emma-watson/61548

Berlatsky, Noah. (2014). A Short History of Male Feminism. *The Atlantic, Politics*. Retrieved from https://www.theatlantic.com/politics/archive/2014/06/a-short-history-of-male-feminism/372673/

The Biography.com website. (2018). "Emmeline Pankhurst Biography". *A&E Television Networks*. Retrieved from https://www.biography.com/people/emmeline-pankhurst-9432764

Chira, Susan and Blaise, Lilia. (2017). France's First Lady, a Confidante and Coach, May Break the Mold. *New York Times, Europe*. Retrieved from https://nyti.ms/2q6FwKv

Fisher, Lauren Alexis. (2017). 25 Inspiring Women Who Shaped Feminism: The women of the 20th and 21st century to celebrate in honor of International Women's Day. *Harper's Bazaar, Features*. Retrieved from http://www.harpersbazaar.com/culture/features/g4201/famous-feminists-throughout-history/

Fleishman, Jeffrey. (Oct. 26, 2015). Poetry is a witness' to suffering wrought by Syria's civil war. *Los Angeles Times*. Retrieved from http://www.latimes.com/world/great-reads/la-ca-c1-syria-war-poetry-20151026-story.html

Foner, Eric and Garraty, John A., Editors. (1991). The Reader's Companion to American History©. *Houghton Mifflin Harcourt Publishing Company*. All rights reserved. Retrieved from http://www.history.com/topics/womens-history/elizabeth-cady-stanton

Joost, Wesley. (PDF) (Sept. 21, 2015). Sing Lesbian Cat, Fly Lesbian Seagull: Interview with Alison Bechdel. *Goblin Magazine*, reprinted in *The Guardsman*. Retrieved from http://www.theguardsman.com/051500/page10.pdf

The Lilith Gallery Network. (2018). *The Art History Archive*. Retrieved from (http://www.arthistoryarchive.com/arthistory/baroque/Artemisia-Gentileschi.html

Mill, John Stuart (2005), The Subjection of Women, in Cudd, Ann E.; Andreasen, Robin O., Feminist theory: a Philosophical Anthology (pp. 17–26). Oxford, UK Malden. Massachusetts: Blackwell Publishing.

National Museum of Women in the Arts. (2018). *Artist Profiles*, Cindy Sherman. Retrieved from https://nmwa.org/explore/artist-profiles/cindy-sherman?gclid=CjwKCAiA8P_TBRA9EiwA-JrpHM-jwfS11JmDawJLnw1zBdm8L6pW9zcu-Dp3JPbjAV17XXfiv9U_Q1xoCeLUQAvD_BwE

Office of Gloria Steinem©. (2018). All rights reserved. Retrieved from http://www.gloriasteinem.com/about/

Woodlief, Ann M. (1994). Biography of Anne Bradstreet. Archived webpage. English Department, Virginia Commonwealth University. Retrieved from https://archive.vcu.edu/english/engweb/webtexts/Bradstreet/bradbio.htm

Youssef, Elyane, Editor: Ramazzina, Yoli. (2018). Waylon H. Lewis Enterprises. Retrieved from https://www.elephantjournal.com/2017/02/frida-kahlo-an-icon-of-feminism-freedom/

ZFS Holdings, LLC. (2017). Retrieved from https://www.hillaryclinton.com/issues

Made in the USA
San Bernardino, CA
01 March 2018